A TECHNIQUE FOR EVALUATING INTERVIEWER PERFORMANCE

CHARLES F. CANNELL
SALLY A. LAWSON
DORIS L. HAUSSER

A Manual for Coding and Analyzing Interviewer Behavior
from Tape Recordings of Household Interviews

Survey Research Center ● Institute for Social Research
The University of Michigan
Ann Arbor, Michigan

ISR Code No. 4022

\

ISBN 0-87944-174-7

Published by the Survey Research Center of the Institute for Social Research,
The University of Michigan, Ann Arbor, Michigan 48106

PREFACE

This manual describes a new coding technique to be used in training and supervising interviewers. Section A, the first of three sections, consists of a single chapter which contains a brief description of the system, including information about its development and the rationale underlying the procedures, the purposes for which it is intended, and the ways in which it has been used.

Section B contains descriptions of the codes, their uses, and the procedures for coding tape-recorded interviews. These chapters are directed toward those who train and supervise coders and those who will use the results for training and supervising interviewers.

Section C consists of sample materials, including a basic, detailed manual (Chapter 7) for coders on coding tape-recorded interviews. This section also contains documentation for the computer program and information for interviewers on the use of tape recorders.

We will appreciate hearing about reactions to the process in practical situations. We are anxious to learn from the experiences of our users, and to make changes in procedures in accordance with their suggestions.

The development of the coding system and the preparation of this manual have been extended over a considerable time, and the finished products represent the contributions of many people. We particularly want to recognize some of the major contributors: Tracy Berckmans and John C. Scott, of the Survey Research Center Field Office suggested many useful ideas for procedures and assisted in the original field studies; Lois Moore and Jacqueline Thorsby did the observational ratings of the interviews; Peter Solenberger prepared the computer program and provided the documentation found in Chapter 11; Morris Klein did much of the statistical analysis. We also want to extend our especial appreciation to those people in the field who recorded their interviews for our use, to the coders who helped us to develop the codes, and to the SRC field supervisors who used preliminary codes to evaluate the strengths and weaknesses of the system. Our thanks also to Alice Sano who typeset the manuscript and to Marlene Ellin who did the final editing.

Financial support for the research, development and preparation of this manual came from two sources:

Bureau of Health Services Research Grant HS00624
National Science Foundation NSF (GI-29904)

October 1974
Ann Arbor

TABLE OF CONTENTS

CHAPTER 1

INTERVIEWER SUPERVISORY TECHNIQUE

INTRODUCTION

This manual describes a new technique for evaluating interviewer performance based on the coding of recordings of interviewer behavior. The system uses codes which encompass all of the interviewer's major verbal activity and is designed for use in both training and on-the-job supervision. For each class of behavior there are codes to evaluate the quality of the interviewer's performance. For example, there are several codes which classify the interviewer's reading of a question: there is a code for questions which he asks correctly and completely, one for those which he asks with minor changes and omissions, and one for those which he either rewords substantially or does not complete.

Overall, the coding system indicates whether questions were asked correctly or incorrectly, whether probes were non-directive or directive, whether responses were summarized accurately or inaccurately, and whether various other behaviors were appropriate or inappropriate. The coded results reflect the degree to which the interviewer employs the methods in which he has been trained. That is, an "incorrect" or "inappropriate" behavior is defined as one which the interviewer has been trained to avoid.

This system is useful in three ways:

1. In initial training, it teaches the novice interviewer which interviewing techniques are acceptable and which are not.

2. It serves as a basis for interviewers and supervisors to review work in the field by coding interviews and discussing the problems which the coding reveals.

3. It provides an assessment of an interviewer's performance, which can be compared both with the performances of other interviewers and with the individual's own performances during other interviews. In order to make such comparisons, the distribution of good and poor behavior for each interviewer is compared with the distribution for all interviewers.

This technique provides objective data for evaluation. It also pinpoints specific instances of inadequate performances on the audio tapes, so that the interviewer and supervisor can listen to each mistake and discuss appropriate corrective measures.

INTERVIEWER SUPERVISORY TECHNIQUE

BACKGROUND

There is abundant evidence that personal interviews are often distorted and invalid and that the interviewer's performance may be responsible for these biases. Most persons who work closely with interviewers are aware of the need for on-the-job supervision, but they have neither the appropriate techniques nor the available time for the type of supervision which would help to insure good performance.

As a consequence, evaluations of interviewers' performances are usually based upon an office review of such factors as response rates, legibility, omissions, uncodable responses and costs, while the techniques which the interviewer used to obtain the responses are largely ignored.

None of these office reviews enables a supervisor to determine whether or not an interviewer has asked the questions correctly, has probed in acceptable ways, or has recorded the answers accurately. H. D. Willcock[1] reports an experiment in which interviewers were observed and evaluated in the field, and the errors listed were compared with those which were found by editing the questionnaires. Only 12% of the errors which were made by the interviewers could be detected through a careful inspection of the questionnaire. The most common of these "invisible errors" were: failure either to probe for additional information or to clarify answers (39%); misclassification of answers in the recording process (22%); the use of incorrect wording or biased probing which altered the scope of a question (19%); and incomplete or inaccurate recording of verbatim answers (11%).

One of our studies of tape recordings showed that 36% of the questions were not asked as written and 20% were altered sufficiently to destroy comparability. Nineteen percent of the probes were directive in nature, which increased the likelihood of biased responses.

If only office supervision is used, interviewers cannot be evaluated on the basis of those behaviors which relate to their most important activity: their use of the questionnaire and the principles of interviewing. This limitation has two undesirable consequences. First, since the interviewer's performance is evaluated only on the basis of selected aspects of his role, any reinforcement is likely to influence the particular behavior which has been reinforced but is not likely to encourage improvement in interviewing techniques generally. Secondly, skill in interviewing is acquired through continual evaluation and feedback. There is evidence which shows that the absence of such feedback results in a lowered level of performance.

---

[1]H. D. Willcock, "Field Observation: A Progress Report." Social Survey Papers, Methodological Series, No. M53 (1952). Reprinted in M. Harris (ed.), *Selected Papers on Interviewers and Interviewing.* London: The Social Survey and J.M.S.O., 1956, pp. 125-131.

4

INTERVIEWER SUPERVISORY TECHNIQUE

We can describe some research findings which show that unreinforced interviewer behavior deteriorates rapidly after training. With reinforcement this deterioration does not occur. In a study of reporting of hospitalizations,[2] a sample of some 2,000 hospital discharge records was obtained. Twenty-seven experienced interviewers called at the home addresses and asked a family member whether anyone in the family had been hospitalized overnight or longer within the past year. The findings showed that the more interviews an interviewer conducted, the less likely it was that the person being interviewed would report the known hospitalization.

In another study of accuracy of reporting physician visits[3] which occurred during the two weeks preceding the interview, a systematic sample was drawn from clinic records of patients. Each week's interviews was an independent random sample of patients who had visited the clinic during the week. Ten inexperienced interviewers were hired and trained for one week. The interviewing extended over five weeks. The percentage of people who failed to report a visit to a physician was 18% for the first week of interviewing and increased steadily (and significantly) to 29% during the fifth week of interviewing.

One other relevant study does not have validity measures. The dependent variable was the number of health conditions and behaviors which were reported. Because the procedures required interviewers to use carefully controlled interviewing techniques, it was necessary to institute special field supervisory procedures. Each interviewer was observed every week during the field work by a supervisor who was present during actual household interviews. Attention was focused on interviewing techniques and each interview was carefully reviewed with the interviewer. In contrast to the findings of other studies, physical conditions, symptoms and physician visits were reported *more* frequently in the second half of the interviewing period than they had been in the first half. Again, a reinforcement interpretation is appropriate. In this study attention was given to the interviewer's technical performance, while in previous studies all of the feedback was focused on the quality of the completed questionnaire. It seems likely that this shift in the focus of attention from the questionnaire to the interviewer's technique increased the interviewers' skills and heightened their motivation to perform adequately. Conversely, when there was no specific feedback on techniques, motivation seemed to diminish, and the number of events reported dropped correspondingly. It is not surprising that an interviewer's lack of incentive or interest in conducting

---

[2]Charles Cannell, Gordon Fisher & Thomas Bakker, Reporting of Hospitalizations in the Health Interview Survey, *Vital and Health Statistics,* U.S. Public Health Service, Series 2, No. 6, July 1965.

[3]C. F. Cannell, and F. G. Fowler, A Study of the Reporting of Visits to Doctors in the National Health Survey. Survey Research Center, University of Michigan 1963. Unpublished report.

an interview results in poor performance, but the rate at which the interviewer's performance appears to drop, according to the findings of these studies, is surprising.

These data with regard to poor interviewer performance led us to consider whether there might be better methods of evaluating and correcting interviewing performance. Essentially, there are three questions which must be considered in any system which evaluates the effectiveness of an interviewer. First, does the interviewer know what constitutes an adequate performance? Second, is the interviewer sufficiently skilled to behave in the correct manner? Third, is the interviewer motivated to perform correctly and adequately? Knowledge of correct behavior is, of course, a major component of the interviewer's training. The principles and techniques which are specified during interviewer training are the "correct" behaviors, so that evaluations of a performance may differ in some respects from one staff to another, depending upon the principles of interviewing which each one teaches or stresses. The appraisal system should then focus on the major behaviors which are taught during training, identify each one, and evaluate its performance.

GOALS OF AN EVALUATION SYSTEM

There are some generally accepted principles which define the goals of an evaluation system which can be used as a frame of reference to describe the interviewer evaluation system in this manual. Briefly, these principles state that:

1. The system should foster a positive supportive relationship between the individual, his supervisor and the organization.

2. The system should be based upon objective and rapid feedback of actual (not role-played) performance.

3. The system should help the individual to perceive his own deficiencies.

4. The system should focus on the behaviors which are most central to and most important for good performance.

5. The system should not be too costly to operate and maintain.

6. The appraisal procedures should not interfere with the interviewer's performance of his interviewing tasks.

The procedure which is usually used, if in fact any system is used for evaluating actual interviewing performance, is some form of field observation in which a supervisor accompanies an interviewer into the household and observes the interview. This procedure is distasteful to the interviewer and disrupting to the interview. Furthermore, since the supervisor must take notes on his observations it is usual to focus on examples of bad performance rather than a more balanced evaluation. The results, thus, tend to appear quite negative with resulting poor morale. It is also an expensive process for a supervisor to spend his time accompanying interviewers as they call on sample houses. The supervisor's efficiency is low and he may spend an entire day and observe only one or two interviews. Finally, there is a problem of reliability of the supervisory observations; especially, there is frequently a lack of agreement between the interviewer and supervisor as to what actually occurred. For these and other reasons, observation of interviewers is frequently not done and if carried out is generally disagreeable for both interviewers and supervisors and disruptive of the interview.

INTERVIEWER REACTIONS TO THE SYSTEM

In an attempt to avoid these problems and to provide a better procedure for evaluating interviewer performance, we developed a technique based on tape recordings of interviews made in respondents' homes. These recordings are coded, with a code which identifies each interviewer behavior as acceptable or unacceptable. This procedure helps to overcome most problems of the observational procedures.

To investigate the effects of this coding, 60 regular sample interviews were recorded and subjected to two procedures:

1. The interviews were evaluated by field supervisors as they would have done in an observational interview in the household.

2. The same interviews were coded using the interviewer behavior code.

This comparison between supervisors' observations of interviewers and coded information on behavior for the same interviews showed great difference, as might be expected, in the quantity of behavior reported. The on-the-spot observations listed an average of 10.4 behaviors per interview, while the codes of the recorded data showed 291.9 behaviors. Another revealing statistic is that of the behaviors recorded in the observations: 13.5% were rated as "good" performances, and 86.5% were rated as "inadequate" performances. The recordings rate 75.5% as "good" performances and 23.5% as "inadequate" performances. It is characteristic of observational evaluative methods to focus on the negative aspects of a performance.

A questionnaire was sent to 112 interviewers on the Survey Research Center staff who had both been observed and had tape recorded actual interviews in order to see how they reacted to each method.

Would you prefer to record interviews or be observed?

Prefer tape recording	40%
No particular preference	29
Prefer observation	26
Don't know	5
	100%

INTERVIEWER SUPERVISORY TECHNIQUE

The questionnaire responses showed that interviewers perceive both observational interviews and recordings as to some extent distracting to both the respondent and the interviewer. Surprisingly, they considered a recording somewhat more distracting to the interviewer than an observer though they considered it the preferable method. The tape recording has several advantages over an observer. Generally, the tape recorder is relatively unobtrusive, since it is small, immobile and silent when it is in operation. Most respondents appear to forget that it is present soon after the interview begins. The most important advantage, however, is that a recording constitutes an exact and complete record of the interview. It can be used to focus attention on specific interviewing techniques and on the detailed interaction between interviewer and respondent. It can be studied and discussed with the interviewer and can be used to illustrate points by reproducing the actual behavior rather than depending upon the observer's memory and thus minimizes disagreements between interviewer and supervisor.

Another of its significant advantages is its salutary effects on the interviewer's morale. As previous data suggest, since an observer can record only a small fraction of the interviewer behavior, he tends to focus on those aspects which need correction. The evaluation feedback session is then essentially negative, focusing on errors and faults. With the recording and coding technique, a better balance is achieved. Unless the interviewer is an absolute failure, "good" behaviors are coded far in excess of the "bad" ones. Feedback can then be more balanced with comments on both positive and negative aspects of the performance so that the interviewer will be less defensive and will have a more positive reaction overall to the evaluation process.

The coding of the interview provides objective measures of the interviewer's performance. The reliability of the coding is high with adequate training. The scores can be used to compare interviewers with each other, to chart the progress of an individual interviewer over time, to evaluate the training program, and to supply indicators for the program's weaknesses.

Usually, the tape recording procedure is cheaper than is the observation method. Once the tape recorders have been purchased, the recordings themselves are inexpensive, since tapes can be reused many times. The biggest cost saving, however, is in terms of supervisors' time. In order to observe household interviews on probability samples, the supervisor must spend a considerable amount of time following the interviewer as he makes fruitless calls at homes whose occupants are absent.

The taping system does have some obvious weaknesses. As in any other evaluative situation the person being recorded is frequently somewhat tense and uneasy about the process, so that the performance may not be as good as it would have been under normal circumstances. Conversely, since the interviewer recognizes the reason for the recording, he will try to exhibit his best performance, which may not be typical of his usual behavior. However, if an interviewer records five or six interviews and the first two are not coded, the initial awkwardness with the recording technique may dissipate and the results may be more representative.

Another weakness of the technique is that the original contact at the respondent's door is not recorded. This is not a technical, but an ethical issue. It is unethical (and perhaps illegal) to record interviews without the subjects' knowledge and permission, and since that is obtained only after an introduction has been made, the initial contact is lost. This omission is unfortunate, since recordings of the initial contact could be useful in improving response rates by helping interviewers to improve their introductory behavior.

Adequate and rapid feedback is necessary for an effective supervisory technique. The feedback from the tape coding method is often not as immediate as with an observer. Several days or weeks may intervene between the recording session and the discussion concerning it. The effect of this delay is partially alleviated by playing back the tape during the review session to recapitulate the original experience.

Another deficiency of the tape is that it cannot record non-verbal behavior. The significance of this omission is difficult to assess. At times non-verbal cues are significant to the interpretation of verbal behavior. It is our subjective impression, however, that even without these cues, the coding procedures are still quite valid.

USE OF BEHAVIOR CODING
IN INTERVIEWER TRAINING

Most interviewer training programs emphasize practice in interviewing rather than listening to lectures about techniques as a means of becoming a competent interviewer. Training usually includes frequent role-playing by the trainees as well as actual household interviewing once the trainee has enough experience and confidence in his ability to conduct an interview.

Practice is effective only if the trainee is aware of and can identify and correct unacceptable behavior. For this reason, a training program usually teaches the trainee to differentiate between good and bad techniques and teaches him the most effective ways in which he can use good techniques. The trainee needs much practice in order to become proficient both in interviewing and in evaluating his own performance. The audio tape and coding system technique is designed to help the novice in these learning processes.

The behavior code identifies and classifies each behavior according to its conformance to, or divergence from, a behavioral principle. All of the major principles of interviewing are operationalized in this way.

9

The coding system is constructed so that it:

1. Includes all concepts and principles which are considered to be important targets in training.

2. Identifies various forms of verbal behavior which are representative of each of these principles.

3. Classifies each behavior as either satisfactory or unsatisfactory according to the principles.

Training in the use of the codes is of major assistance in familiarizing the trainee with the principles of interviewing, in helping him to differentiate adequate from inadequate behavior, and in providing him continuous evaluations of his own performance. Self-coding provides the trainee with regular and frequent reinforcement.

The tape recorder should be introduced very early in the training sessions, so that its strangeness and the potential threat of the recording procedure will have dissipated by the time actual field interviewing begins. There are several ways in which recordings are useful in training. When the interviewer first starts to practice interviewing (usually within the training group) he can make use of the codes as he listens to his own interviews. Role-playing interviews are usually conducted in groups of three with one person acting as the observer or evaluator. The observer can use the codes as a basis for his feedback to the interviewer. As training progresses, the trainer or supervisor can code selected interviews both to assist in training the interviewer and to obtain a basis for determining the point at which the interviewer has achieved an acceptable level of performance for production interviewing.

USE OF CODES BY SUPERVISORS

Supervisors can use the codes to reinforce the training of both new and experienced interviewers and to identify and correct weaknesses in their performance. Supervisors have found that by listening to tapes together with the interviewer, coding and discussing as they proceed, they can increase the interviewer's involvement in the process and provide immediate feedback for each performance.

The supervisor can also code parts of several interviews conducted by each person in order to ascertain whether their errors are consistent over a number of respondents or whether they are the idiosyncrasies of a particular respondent or interview situation.

OFFICE CODING AND SUPERVISION

For a larger interviewing staff which requires supervision over a long period of time it is more efficient and less expensive to employ trained coders to code the tapes than for the supervisors to do their own coding. A computer program is available for handling the variable length records of behaviors; it converts them into a format in which the OSIRIS system (available from the Institute for Social Research) or other statistical programs can be used. The output can then be sent to the supervisor.

EVALUATING THE ACCURACY OF THE INTERVIEW CONTENT

These tape recordings can be used to determine the degree of accuracy with which the interviewer recorded the respondents' replies. This can be done by applying the same content code to the written interview report and then to the tape recording. The discrepancies indicate the number and types of errors which the interviewer made when he was writing up the interview.

FLEXIBILITY OF THE CODES

The codes which are presented in this manual are consistent with a particular set of interviewing principles and techniques. These techniques are widely applicable not only to survey research interviewing, but also to other types of interviews. The code categories can be changed, expanded, depleted, and adapted to fit particular needs. It is essential, however, that the behavior which is to be coded be clearly and uniquely described, so that coding decisions can be made with high reliability.

If the codes are to be used for non-survey interviews, they will require considerable alteration. Survey research uses fixed questions, and the codes which relate to behavior in question asking are designed with this in mind. New evaluative categories would be required for interviews in which the interviewer also frames the questions. The principles, however, are generally consistent for all types of interviewing because all interviewers attempt to obtain unbiased responses. The interviewer behaviors shown here then, are applicable to a wide range of interview types and this system should be useful in training and evaluating interviewers in fields such as medicine, law, journalism, and social work.

The remainder of the manual describes the procedures and uses of this system in training and supervising interviewers. It describes the codes, the coding process and uses of the coded data in the detail necessary for someone planning to use this technique.

CHAPTER 2

THE INTERVIEWER BEHAVIOR CODE[1]

Before the procedure for using the behavior code can be described (Chapter 4), some explanation of the code itself is necessary. The coding system is organized around the following interviewer activities: (a) asking the question, (b) probing for adequate responses, (c) providing clarification about the question, (d) general activities, such as giving the respondent feedback, (e) non-recorded activities, such as omitting a question because of a skip pattern on the questionnaire, and (f) mentioning the study background. The system also considers the pace at which the interview is conducted and the interviewer's voice inflection. The codes are grouped into numerical clusters according to these types of behaviors. The chart below shows this system of organization.

Organization of Code

10's - Correct Question

Question read correctly or with slight change which does not alter frame of reference.

20's - Incorrect Question

Question read incorrectly, and frame of reference distorted, or question read that should have been skipped.

30's - Appropriate Probes

Non-directive probes and clarifications which effect no limitation or change in either frame of reference or potential response.

40's - Inappropriate Probes

Directive probes and clarifications which either limit or change the frame of reference of the question or response.

50's - Other Appropriate Behavior

Helping behaviors such as feedback which do not jeopardize validity by influencing the respondent.

60's - Other Inappropriate Behavior

Behaviors which may jeopardize validity by influencing the respondent, such as giving opinions or interrupting.

---

[1] Supervisors or trainers should study all of Section B, while the persons they then train in the use of the code might need only Chapter 7, the Coder Manual.

THE INTERVIEWER BEHAVIOR CODE

70's - Non-Recorded Behavior
Non-verbal behavior, such as question skipped or no sound on tape

80's - Pace and Voice Inflection
Speed of interviewer pace and voice inflection.

90's - Study Background
Information concerning background and intent of study.

The following chart is a brief introduction to each of the individual codes within this framework. (For a more complete discussion of these codes, the reader should refer to Chapter 7, a manual designed for use during coding, which contains more elaborate descriptions and examples of the behaviors in each category, along with rules for making choices among similar codes.)

Category	Code	Used When the Interviewer . . .
1 - Asks question as printed	11	reads question exactly as printed on the questionnaire
	12	reads question making minor modifications of the printed version, but does not alter frame of reference
2 - Asks question incorrectly	21	reads main stem of question as printed, but modifies or incorrectly reads any response categories in the question (does not apply therefore to open questions, since they do not have response categories)
	22	either significantly alters main body or stem of question while reading it, or reads only part of it
	23	does not read question, but instead makes a statement about the response he anticipates
	27	asks a question which should have been skipped
3 - Probes or clarifies non-directively	31	makes up in own words a probe (query) which is non-directive
	32	repeats printed question or part of it correctly
	34	repeats respondent's response, or part of it, correctly
	35	confirms a frame of reference for respondent correctly and in a non-directive manner
4 - Probes or clarifies directively	41	makes up a probe which is directive, limiting or changing the frame of reference of either the question or the potential response
	42	either repeats question and/or response choices incorrectly or gives incorrect summary of respondent's response
	43	gives an introduction which is directive
	45	either interprets question by rewording it or confirms a frame of reference incorrectly

THE INTERVIEWER BEHAVIOR CODE

Category	Code	Used When the Interviewer . . .
5 - Other appropriate behavior	51	helps respondent to understand his role, for example by task-oriented clarification
	58	exhibits other acceptable behavior, such as volunteering general feedback
6 - Other inappropriate behavior	62	interrupts respondent
	63	gives personal opinion or evaluation
	67	records response incorrectly or incompletely on questionnaire
	68	exhibits other unacceptable behavior
7 - Non-recorded	71	omits question correctly (due to skip pattern)
	72	omits question incorrectly
	73	writes in inferred or previously obtained answer
	75	fails to probe after inadequate answer
	78	missing data, no sound on tape
8 - Pace and voice inflection	81	reads question more slowly than 2 words/sec.
	82	reads question at 2 words/sec.
	83	reads question more quickly than 2 words/sec
	84	conducts entire interview too slowly
	85	conducts entire interview at right pace
	86	conducts entire interview too quickly than 2 words/sec.
	87	reads questions in a wooden, expressionless manner
	88	reads questions with a rising inflection at the end
	89	reads questions with voice dropped, so that they sound like a statement
9 - Background of study	91	mentions own name
	92	mentions sponsorship
	93	mentions anonymity
	94	mentions respondent selection procedures
	95	mentions purpose of study

If it is desired, the code scheme may be reduced to a single digit. That is, instead of codes 11 and 12, the code 1 could be used for both of these behaviors, the code 2 could be used for all behaviors in the 20's and so on. This method facilitates more rapid coding, but it reduces the amount of information which is obtained for analysis, and the evaluative information becomes more limited. The table below outlines this alternative version of the code.

Reduced Code

Code	Definition
1 - Correct Question Asking	Interviewer reads question either exactly as printed on the questionnaire or with minor modifications which do not alter the frame of reference
2 - Incorrect Question Asking	Interviewer either significantly alters part of question, or omits part of question, or replaces question with own statement, or reads question which should have been skipped
3 - Probes or Clarifies Non-directively	Interviewer either makes up in own words a probe which is non-directive, repeats all or part of either question or respondent's answer in a non-directive manner, or confirms a frame of reference for respondent correctly
4 - Probes or Clarifies Directively	Interviewer either makes up probe which is directive, repeats question or respondent's answer incorrectly, gives a directive introduction, or confirms a frame of reference incorrectly
5 - Other Appropriate Behavior	Interviewer gives either acceptable task-oriented clarification or other appropriate feedback
6 - Other Inappropriate Behavior	Interviewer either interrupts respondent, or gives personal opinion, or records responses incorrectly on questionnaire
7 - Non-recorded Activity	Interviewer either omits a question, or there is missing data
8 - Pace	Interviewer conducts interview either too slowly or too rapidly
9 - Background of Study	Interviewer mentions own name, study sponsorship, respondent selection, anonymity, purpose of study

(Expanded definitions of these categories are found in the Coder's Manual, Chapter 7)

In addition to the behaviors which are included in the code scheme, there are a few interviewer behaviors which are left uncoded. For instance, comments which relate to interviewing equipment, such as, "here's a blue card" are not coded, because interviewers who use gestures would be disadvantaged. Also, if an introduction to a question or section is optional, it is not coded unless the introduction is inappropriate. Brief acceptable feedback such as "Uh-huh" is not coded. However, if the brief feedback is in the form of complete words or phrases such as "I see," "Thank you," "Fine," it is coded. Finally, conversations which occur between the interviewer and some third person in the room who is not a respondent are not coded.

The trainer or supervisor should review the questionnaire which is being coded in order to determine whether there are any questions which require exceptional treatment. In particular, the following steps must be performed.

THE INTERVIEWER BEHAVIOR CODE

1. Check all questions for parenthetical remarks. Indicate for the coder whether or not the interviewer is required to read them, and whether or not the interviewer is allowed to make any substitutions in the wording.
2. In each question, circle any words that may be left out of an "exact" reading ("exact" means that the coder may code the reading, code 11).
3. Underline or note any words which may be either added or omitted for a code 12 (question slightly modified) on each question.
4. Place parentheses around any part of a question which the interviewer is not required to read.

If the supervisor follows these steps, the coders can then be consistent when they evaluate the degree of correctness with which interviewers read the question.

CODING DISCRETION

Coding is used to classify appropriate and inappropriate behaviors. The odd-numbered categories represent those behaviors which are considered appropriate in accordance with the principles of general interviewing theory, while even-numbered categories represent inappropriate behaviors. The standards that were employed in designing the code and which are clearly reflected in the definitions of the code categories, were derived from existing principles of interviewing which have been generally accepted and stressed in training.

It is possible to develop some generalized standards for acceptability and correctness which differ from those which are implicit in this coding system. Because the code distinguishes between acceptable and unacceptable versions of the same behavior, anyone who uses the code may either re-define categories or change particular examples if they wish. There are some instances in which the questionnaire in use may make this desirable. If a questionnaire is written so that it requires many very specific answers, the researchers may consider it appropriate to probe in a more directive manner than is customary in order to obtain the required information. For such a questionnaire, the coder could be instructed to be more generous in his use of non-directive categories in the 30's.

Generally, the codes in the 50's and 60's are most open to interpretation. For instance, if in a particular study the interviewers were instructed to maintain a professional demeanor, then coders could be instructed to be very restrictive in their use of 50's codes when the interviewer behaved in a casual manner. This type of change in the coding interpretation would usually be anticipated in the case of special studies for which the interviewer has been instructed to behave in a manner which differs from the behavior he has been taught in traditional training sessions.

A final factor which determines the assignment of codes to behaviors is the general level or degree of stringency which will be applied to the criteria for all codes. For instance, at one degree of rigor, the code category (12), for cases in which the question is asked with a slight change which does not alter the frame of reference, may be defined very narrowly, so that if the question as asked deviates *at all* from the printed question, a code from the 20 series (question asked incorrectly) will be assigned. The resulting data would then reflect a perfection/something-other-than-perfection dichotomy, rather than a continuum from perfection through minor changes to major changes. Likewise, the definition of "appropriate" behavior may be more or less rigorous for all of the individual codes. Because the degree of severity with which the coder approaches his task does affect the outcome of the coding procedure, it is essential that this variable be given considerable attention. Each time the code is used, whether it be for a one-time examination of a group of interviewers in order to determine trouble spots in the pre-test of a questionnaire, or whether it be for a long-term interviewer evaluation program, users of the coded data must agree on the level of stringency that is desired.

For example, a researcher conducting a survey which uses a series of questions being repeated from earlier studies may want some data to indicate the reliability of that replication. To obtain these data, he could define 'question asked correctly' to mean '*no* deviation from the question as printed' (or any other definition, as long as it is comparable and reliable). This degree of stringency could be restricted only to those questions which are being replicated; it need not cover the entire survey. Likewise, it may be desired for a variety of reasons to allow a very broad range of alteration for particular questions. The Coder Manual in Chapter 7 employs a high level of stringency, and reflects the professional manner one expects of interviewers.

In summary, special standards of judgment and any exceptional cases must be identified so that the more general coding can be adapted to them in order to increase coder objectivity and the reliability of the data. It is our impression that more stringent definitions provide greater clarity in the coding task and increase the reliability of the data. In addition, it appears that the more thorough definitions (regardless of the level of stringency) facilitate greater reliability among coders.

CHAPTER 3

MAKING THE TAPE RECORDINGS

The first step in the behavior coding process is obtaining the tape-recorded interviews. In a typical situation, the interviewer carries a small cassette tape recorder to the interview. Ideally the machine is equipped with a self-contained microphone and can operate on batteries; these features help to minimize the time and effort required to set up the machine for recording and eliminate the possibility of misplacing accessories.

The interviewer makes his usual doorstep introduction, identifying himself and explaining the purpose of the interview. Only after the respondent has agreed to be interviewed does the interviewer introduce the tape recorder. He explains that it is standard procedure to tape record interviews and that if there are no objections, he would like to record this one. If necessary, he may add a comment about wanting to insure that the respondent's answers and opinions are recorded accurately. The respondent has the right either to refuse to tape the interview or to ask that the taping be stopped at any point during the interview. However, of several hundred respondents whom we have interviewed, only a few said they preferred not to have the interview recorded.

Some interviewers are concerned that the presence of the tape recorder may exert a negative influence upon respondents. Some respondents, they feel, withhold information when the tape recorder is present, and occasionally report additional information after the interview because they do not want it to be recorded. A study by Belson[1] showed no significant differences between interviews which were recorded and those which were not, although there were some indications of differences according to the socio-economic status of the respondent. Also, factors such as the degree of difficulty of the recall task required for responding and the degree of personal information which the questions demand may have an effect on the accuracy of responses made during tape-recorded interviews. More systematic research needs to be conducted in order to determine the extent of any effect which the presence of the tape recorder may have on the accuracy and quality of responses.

---

[1] Belson, William A. Tape Recordings—Its Effect on Accuracy of Response in Survey Interviews. *Journal of Marketing Research*, Vol. 4, Issue 3, August 1967.

It appears that the interviewer can help to eliminate any hesitancy on the part of the respondent. It is essential that the interviewer have a working knowledge of the recorder and its maintenance requirements. (See Chapter 10 for sample instructions.) Instructions for operating a particular machine are supplied by the manufacturer upon purchase. The interviewer should use a tape recorder throughout his initial training, so that it becomes as much a part of his interviewing technique as does the interview schedule. If the interviewer is comfortable with the machine, has no difficulty in setting it up, and generally behaves as though taping were a standard interviewing procedure, the respondent accepts this, shows little reluctance, and soon forgets that the tape recorder is there. At the end of the interview, when the interviewer stops the recording process, respondents are often interested in hearing their own voices, and interviewers frequently play back part of the recording for the respondent's amusement.

The tape recording is then sent either to a central office or to a supervisor to be coded. When the tape recording is received at a central point, it is logged in and given an identification number. A record is made of this number, the interviewer, the particular study for which this interview was conducted, the interviewer's interview number, and the identification number of the questionnaire which corresponds to that interview. After this, the tape can be coded by a central staff, and the results can be returned to the supervisor for evaluation.

A FEW COMMENTS ON CASSETTE TAPES, TAPE RECORDERS AND PLAY-BACK MACHINES

We will not attempt to provide a complete technical evaluation of available equipment, but we did discover early that poor tapes and poor equipment are a great nuisance, as well as a waste of time and money. The following describes our experiences with selected equipment.

Cassette Recorders

We tried several models and types of cassette recorders. We found the most satisfactory to be the Sony TC-110; it is light, and its carrying case with shoulder strap makes it easy to transport. The Sony had fewer breakdowns and malfunctions than did any other model. The prices of recorders varied at the time of our comparisons; the TC-110 was the model we chose as best suited to our needs and budget. Sony model numbers change each time a very minor change is made. Since the quality of the TC-110 appeared to be commensurate with that of the more expensive models, it would be wise to ask for the current model which most resembles the TC-110.

MAKING THE TAPE RECORDINGS

The important features of the TC-110 for recording interviews in the home are:

1. It can operate on regular household current or batteries. Also, special rechargeable battery packs are available and are most satisfactory. Recordings in the home are made on battery power, in order to avoid the fuss of locating an electric outlet in the respondent's home. Battery packs can be charged each night by plugging the machine into household current.
2. Automatic volume control is particularly important since it permits recordings of either loud or soft voices with no need for adjustment by the interviewer.
3. The machine has a built-in microphone. However, we prefer the remote, non-directional mike which is included with the machine. The built-in mike seems to pick up noise from the machine itself, and the separate mike is more discreet because it can be placed conveniently between the interviewer and respondent with the recorder itself out of the range of vision.

Cassette Tapes

Early experience showed that some tapes were more likely than others to break, tangle, or stretch. There are three brands of tapes, however, which were not prone to these problems: TDK, Maxell, and BASF. Each of these brands has several types of cassette. The "low-noise" type is best for interviewing. With these cassettes, 60 or 90 minute lengths were quite satisfactory, but the 120 minute tapes tended to break or jam and were not satisfactory.

Play-Back Equipment

In order to code from tapes, there must be some method of stopping and reversing the tape. A foot-pedal attachment which leaves the hands free is found only on dictating-type machines, which are considerably more expensive than the recorders described above. The Norelco play-back performed well mechanically and also had excellent sound quality and discrimination ability. These are particularly important considerations when the coding is extensive since they reduce coder fatigue.

The more expensive Sony tape recorders have a replay key which can be depressed without being locked into position, so that the tape can be played slowly. These machines are quite satisfactory for coding, but they are not as convenient as the foot-pedal model.

Since, in our set-up, more than one coder is working at a time, we use earphones. Those which have soft padded or air-filled ear cushions are light and comfortable. They also screen out extraneous environmental sounds, so that the recording is more audible.

MAKING THE TAPE RECORDINGS

Erasing Tapes

Although the cassette recorder has an "erase" head which erases previous sounds just prior to recording so that manual pre-erasing is supposed to be unnecessary, at times the original recording can be heard faintly in the background. This makes an interview which is not recorded under ideal conditions difficult to code at times. A small, inexpensive bulk tape eraser provides a much cleaner tape for re-use.

CHAPTER 4

THE CODING PROCESS

CODER TRAINING[1]

Coder trainees should first study the section of the manual (Chapter 7) which defines the behavior code categories. That chapter contains detailed explanations of the rules governing the code categories and examples of their assignment. It should be used throughout training and retained by each coder for later reference.

After the trainees have studied the manual, more intensive training should be conducted in a group setting, with discussions led by a trainer. The group training should progress through several phases: each phase should focus upon a cluster of related codes and begin with a group discussion of those codes. After this discussion, the group should listen to a taped interview while following along in a questionnaire, and each trainee should record code assignments as he listens, choosing from the codes which the group has just discussed. These code assignments should then be discussed by the group, and any discrepancies in the assignments should be examined.

DEMONSTRATION TAPE

A demonstration tape should be made which covers each phase of the training scheme, providing examples of the behaviors under discussion. The phases should progress from frequent to infrequent codes; frequent codes which are more easily defined and understood should be explained and demonstrated before the less frequent and less comprehensible codes are demonstrated. The code subsets should be introduced in approximately this order: 10's, 30's, 20's, 40's, 50's, 60's, 90's, 70's, with the pace codes (80's) introduced at the very end.

Two persons and a tape recorder are needed to make the demonstration tape. One person should play the role of interviewer and the other the role of respondent. They should record a simulated interview, using the questionnaire which is being used in training. The behavior in the recording should follow

---

[1]This section assumes the availability of a trainer who has read this entire manual, and mastered the code.

the sequence described in the previous paragraph. For the first three or four questions, the interviewer should read the questions either perfectly or with only minor modifications (calling for codes in the 10's), while the respondent gives complete responses. Then for the next few questions, the respondent should give less than complete answers, so that the interviewer must probe, using behaviors described in the 30's. The demonstration interview should proceed in this manner until all of the behaviors included in the code have been encompassed. This type of phased introduction to the code gives the coders an early successful experience in assigning the easier, more frequent codes before they attempt the more difficult code assignments.

For the next phase of the group training session, the trainer should play one or two questions at a time from a tape of an actual production interview for which the trainees have questionnaires. This represents a more natural behavior sequence. The trainees should assign code categories to each section of the interview they hear, and disagreements should again be resolved through group discussion.

INDEPENDENT CODING

Next, all trainees should independently code pre-selected tapes. Several tapes may be used, but each one should be coded independently by at least two trainees. The tapes which are used for this purpose should have good sound reproduction, and should be smooth interviews conducted by well-trained interviewers with a co-operative respondent. Again, these qualities will facilitate a trainee's success in his first attempt at independent coding.

After the trainee has coded two tapes, each set of codes should be compared in its entirety with those of another trainee who coded the same interview. Disagreements can be resolved by playing the tape again. The trainer settles disagreements which are not clearly or accurately resolved by the trainees. The trainer should keep a record of each trainee's "percent agreement," that is, the proportion of the cases in which the trainee had initially assigned the correct code. (This proportion is obtained by dividing the number of correct codes by the total number of codes used in the interview. The trainer has the final authority in determining the correct code when there is a disagreement.)

If a trainee has obtained 80% agreement or better with the final resolution code on the first two tapes which he codes independently, he is ready to begin production coding. Trainees who do not reach this rate of agreement should continue to code tapes and compare codes until they reach 80% agreement on two successive tapes.

In our experience, the time required to train coders initially averages around 15 hours. A complete novice may take as many as 20 hours to train, but coders who are experienced in either content coding or other forms of behavior coding also often require additional time because they have some difficulty "unlearning" old procedures. After an initial "warm-up" period, however, there are no significant differences in the amounts of time which previously experienced coders and previously inexperienced coders require to code tapes.

STUDY-SPECIFIC BRIEFING

Before production coding for any study can begin, coders must be briefed on any particular exceptions to the coding rules in use, and also on whatever general rules regarding acceptability may be in force for that study. If a prescribed schedule of questions was used in the interview (a questionnaire), each coder should be given his own copy on which he may make notes about specific coding exceptions, acceptable rewordings, etc. (as described in Chapter 2). This questionnaire should then be used as a reference in assigning the codes.

PLAYBACK EQUIPMENT

Each coder should use a playback machine with a comfortable set of earphones. The machine does not need to have a recording capability, but it should be designed to facilitate easy, trouble-free playing, rewinding, and stopping, since coding sometimes requires repeated play-replay-stop action.

CODING SHEETS

Each coder should have pre-numbered coding sheets on which the code entries can be made. The coding sheet should be numbered to correspond to the printed questions on the interview schedule and should use numeric notations only to facilitate computer processing. Table 4-1 is an example of part of a code sheet. See Chapter 8 for a completed code sheet.

Table 4-1

Sample Code Sheet

Study No._____   Interviewer No._____   Interview No._____

Quest. No.	Behavior Codes							
1.0								
1.1								
1.2								
2.0								
2.1								
2.2								
2.3								

THE CODING PROCESS

Each horizontal line on the code sheet corresponds to one printed question. The vertical lines represent some *respondent* behavior (which is not coded, of course) as it occurs between interviewer behaviors. If several interviewer behaviors occur without any respondent behavior interspersed, all of the interviewer behavior codes should be entered in the same space (or box) on the sheet. These lines can be used to ascertain at a glance whether a particular behavior occurred at the interviewer's initiative or in response to some behavior by the respondent.

Example

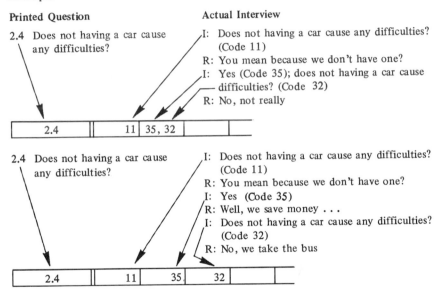

Printed Question   Actual Interview

2.4 Does not having a car cause   I: Does not having a car cause any difficulties?
     any difficulties?   (Code 11)
                                                   R: You mean because we don't have one?
                                                   I: Yes (Code 35); does not having a car cause
                                                      difficulties? (Code 32)
                                                   R: No, not really

| 2.4 | | 11 | 35, 32 | | |

2.4 Does not having a car cause   I: Does not having a car cause any difficulties?
     any difficulties?   (Code 11)
                                                   R: You mean because we don't have one?
                                                   I: Yes (Code 35)
                                                   R: Well, we save money . . .
                                                   I: Does not having a car cause any difficulties?
                                                      (Code 32)
                                                   R: No, we take the bus

| 2.4 | | 11 | 35 | 32 | |

If more interviewer/respondent interactions occur in relation to a single question than there are spaces provided, the spaces may be subdivided with vertical lines.

Example:

| 2.8 | | 11 | 35 | 32,51 | 31 / 31 | 31 / 31 |

Likewise, if an interviewer engages in more behaviors than will fit in one space, without any intervening respondent behavior, a vertical line can be cancelled by lining it out.

Example:

| 2.9 | | 33, | 11 | 62, 34, | 32, 51 | 58 |

28

THE CODING PROCESS

CHECK CODING

Once production coding begins, check coding should be performed in order to establish and maintain a high level of coding reliability. For each interview which is coded, a second coder should independently code 20% of that interview. When a standardized interview schedule is used, the portions of the tape which cover every fifth page of the questionnaire should be check coded; the starting page should be chosen randomly. Since interviewer and respondent styles both vary greatly, it is advisable to check code in this manner, rather than simply to check every fifth interview.

When both sets of codes are available for an interview, a supervisor should tally the two sets and compute a reliability figure. Disagreements concerning the codes assigned should be resolved by the supervisor, who should listen to those precise portions of the interview which caused the discrepancies. If there are systematic patterns of disagreement, the supervisor should discuss the errors with whichever coder has been making them. The individual feedback to each coder which this check coding system generates should help to maintain acceptable levels of performance and prevent either any "coding drift" or the occurrence of unintentional changes in the decision rules. The time required for production coding and check coding should average about 2.5 hours for a 45 minute interview. In addition, code sheets must be keypunched and verified. This involves considerable additional time, but we hope to develop a more efficient system similar to the Optical Character Recognition System.

CODING RELIABILITY

Reliability scores should be computed on a code-by-code basis for each interview by calculating the percentage of agreement, as described earlier. In this way, the percentage of agreement between coders on each individual code, as well as on the total code, can be obtained for each interview.

Using these methods of coder training, check coding, and reliability scoring, the overall reliability scores which have been obtained range from 80% to 92%. These figures compare favorably with other reports of reliability in coding complex behavior.

Disagreements often focus not upon which of two codes should be used for a behavior, but rather upon whether or not a particular behavior should be coded at all. The coding scheme does not uniquely identify a "unit of behavior." Unfortunately, the accommodations which have been made for this uncertainty in other coding procedures, such as coding the activity which is predominant in a prescribed time period, are unsuitable for this system because it is most desirable to try to code *all* of the behaviors which occur, sometimes almost simultaneously, during an interview. The absence of a defined behavior unit, then, will be a common cause of coding disagreements.

COMPUTER PROCESSING

After production coding and check coding are completed, the identifying information and behavior codes from the coding sheets should be prepared for computer input. For each interview, there should be an identification card and one card for each question in the interview (including all skipped questions), which contains the codes for all of the behaviors which occurred in relationship to that question. These data should then be transferred to computer tapes. Presently, these tapes can be processed using a program which is available for use on an IBM 360/40. Chapter 11 contains the set-up and other specifications for this program. Since a wide range of possible uses of any data from the coding system was anticipated, the computer program incorporates a great deal of flexibility in output formats. The appropriate format is determined by the character of the intended use of the data.

When the behavior data are ready to be reported to the interviewer, the computer output and the tape recordings on which the data are based should be returned to the interviewer or his supervisor. The determination as to which individual should review which data should be governed by the specific form and purpose of the feedback in any individual situation. Some possibilities for the disposition of the data are described in the section on feedback.

If only a few interviews have been coded, computer processing is not necessary. The individual codes can be tallied by hand and converted to percentages of total behavior. This is a useful method when a supervisor is coding only one or two interviews to review an interviewer's current performance.

CHAPTER 5

INTERVIEWER TRAINING AND SUPERVISION

Interviewers are introduced to the behavior code early in their training so that they can use the code for evaluating their own performance. Prior to their first role-played (practice) interviews, instructions on the use of the code are given. Following that, the role-played interviews are recorded and the participants (the observer, the interviewer and the respondent) all code the interview. Any coding differences are discussed with the trainer. This process helps the participants to understand the codes. In later role-played interviews, the trainer codes the interviews and uses the codes as a basis for discussions of interviewing techniques, focusing on errors which occur at this stage of training. This method serves three purposes: first, it enables the interviewers to identify and classify each behavior; second, it enables them to differentiate good from bad techniques; and third, it supplies the interviewers with immediate feedback.

An assistant trainer (or a coding clerk) can do the actual coding so that the trainer will be free for other training activities. At the end of training, however, the interviewer should understand the code and have experience in using it, so that he can code his own interviews during actual field work.

INTERVIEWER CODING

As they begin their field work, interviewers should be encouraged to listen to and code portions of their first interviews. Many early problems are caused neither by ignorance of acceptable techniques nor by an inability to recognize good techniques, but rather by a lack of skill and experience in using proper techniques during the stress of the interview. In many cases, the interviewer can simply hear his own mistakes on tape and then avoid making the same errors in future interviews.

DIAGNOSING INTERVIEWING PROBLEMS

The computer output of the behavior data, or a hand-calculated version, constitutes the basic information which should be used to identify both general and specific interviewing problems, and is therefore the basic information which should be available for feedback to interviewers. The computer can provide percentages, distributions of each behavior code for each interview, and a summary of averages both for all interviews and for individual interviews.

The average of all interviewers should be obtained so that each interviewer's performance can be compared with those of others. Averages should be calculated for each study since the form, type, and level of difficulty of a particular questionnaire will change the behavior profiles. There are no standards available for use in evaluating the proportion of behavior in each class, but the reasons for individual averages which deviate markedly from the total averages should be determined. For example, a low percentage figure on probes may indicate that the interviewer is doing an inadequate job of obtaining full responses, but may also indicate that the interviewer has a particularly cooperative respondent. Information such as that contained in Table 5-1 (see page 36 is used primarily as an indicator of potential difficulties for interviewers whose percentages vary markedly from the average.

Table 5-2 (see page 37) provides information for more specific evaluations of performance. Averages can be examined for groups of codes which represent appropriate and inappropriate performances, and if appropriate behaviors are low, individual codes within each group can be examined in order to isolate the difficulty. In this table particularly, the range is important in identifying potential problems. If there is a high proportion of inappropriate behavior for one or more interviews, even if the overall average for that behavior is at a satisfactory level, one should attempt to ascertain the reason for the deviation. The computer output for the particular deviant interview should be examined to see whether or not the pattern suggests a difficult respondent. If the interviewer has other interviews with the same kind of respondent, one can also examine the output for these interviews. The output may indicate either that the respondent was uniquely difficult (low intelligence, very negative, language problem, etc.) or it may indicate that the interviewer normally has trouble with a particular type of respondent. Some interviewers, for example, have difficulty with respondents whose social or educational classes differ markedly from their own.

Another technique which is useful in diagnosing potential problems is to look through the coding sheets for the deviant items to see whether the problems are associated with particular kinds of questions; for example, open or multiple choice formats, questions with complex phrasing, etc.

In order to provide complete feedback to an interviewer, the supervisor should identify the activity he wishes to discuss with the interviewers, and then identify particular examples of that inadequate behavior on the code sheets, circling the corresponding question numbers in color. The supervisor should use the tapes of those interviews to demonstrate the sections which were coded as inadequate, and then discuss techniques which could be used to improve the interviewer's performance. The supervisor should also provide the interviewer with detailed copies of the codes so that he will recognize the activity and the way in which it was coded.

DIAGNOSING PROCEDURES

In order for feedback to be an effective tool for improving performance, the interviewer must know why he performed inadequately. There are at least three major situations which produce inadequate performances:

1. The interviewer does not know what constitutes an adequate performance. The training has not been successful in communicating the theory or concepts which he can use to evaluate his performance.

2. The interviewer may understand the *principles* of good performance but not be able to determine whether or not a particular behavior conforms to those principles. For example, he may not be able to differentiate directive (inappropriate) from non-directive (appropriate) probes, or he may fail to read the alternatives in the question properly because he did not recognize them as part of the question. In both of these instances, the interviewer knows the correct principle, but he cannot distinguish between behavior which does or does not conform to that principle.

3. The interviewer knows the principle, and can distinguish between adequate and inadequate performances, but he still lacks skill in performance. This situation is of course characteristic of new interviewers, but it also sometimes plagues experienced interviewers who have not been active for some time, and those who lack poise or are ill at ease and feel pressured during the interview. As was mentioned earlier, however, this situation may explain an interviewer's behavior only with particular kinds of respondents.

Some insight into the reasons for inadequate performances can be obtained by examining the information in the tables, the computer output for individual interviewers, etc. Most of the information, however, must be obtained from the interviewer as part of the feedback.

The supervisor should play several short segments of tapes which contain examples of inadequate behavior and ask the interviewer to identify any poor performance he recognizes. If he does identify the poor performance, he should then be asked to explain his criteria for the evaluation. His answers should provide the basis for a diagnosis. A new interviewer or a particularly poor interviewer may find this process threatening, but for most experienced interviewers there is a great deal of adequate behavior which can be pointed out at the beginning of the feedback session. This allows the supervisor to focus upon inadequate behavior, but to maintain it in perspective so that it does not become too threatening.

THE FEEDBACK PROCESS

We will not discuss general principles of feedback, but only mention a few specific techniques which are germane to this special situation. It is less threatening to the interviewer, and therefore more effective, if he identifies his own inadequate performances, indicates his recognition of the difficulties, and suggests his own corrective measures. Samples of the code sheets and the original tape recordings of problem interviews should be used, and the interviewer should listen to the tapes and analyze his own behaviors. The supervisor should help to identify problems on the tapes and assist the interviewer both in making a correct assessment of each problem and in formulating a solution to correct it. Retraining then would be an integral part of the feedback process.

USE OF PERFORMANCE DATA OVER TIME

Ideally, feedback should enable the interviewer to formulate goals for his future performances. At the end of each session, the supervisor should encourage the interviewer to pay particular attention to the problems they have just discussed in his next interviews, then keep track of his improvements using the space provided in the two feedback tables. Because the code is based on behaviors which should be used in any interviewing situation, the performance data which the code generates can be compared over time and across studies. An interviewer's performance can be examined as he either improves or maintains desired standards of behavior in accordance with goals which may be formulated at one feedback session. Once each goal has been met, it is still necessary to examine behaviors in order to insure that the target performance is maintained and to insure that other desirable behaviors have not suffered because of the attention to the target behavior.

EXAMPLES OF FEEDBACK TO INTERVIEWERS

The following discussion demonstrates the actual use of the system with two interviewers. One is Interviewer Number 2 (from Tables 9-3 and 9-4 in Chapter 9), and the other is a new interviewer (see Tables 5-3 and 5-4 for data). In both cases, the interviewers are part of a national staff and live some distance from the research center. Each has a regional supervisor who is responsible for their training and supervision, and who receives copies of these tables. Alice Jones' (the new interviewer) supervisor has been alerted to Alice's need for immediate additional training.

Mary Smith (Tables 5-1 and 5-2) appears to be a good interviewer. She does somewhat less probing than the average interviewer and considerably less than she has done in previous performances. However, she seems to do an adequate amount of probing for these interviews. The interviews analyzed here were conducted with highly educated respondents whose generally superior performance decreased the need for probing. The interviewer asked questions well

(Table 5-1), improving considerably since her previous performance. Her major problem was that she asked questions too quickly, and tended to rush into the next question without giving the respondent adequate time to reply. She was told to consult the section of her *Interviewer's Manual*[1] which discusses the interview pace. Since her performance was generally good, the tapes of her interviews were not returned to her for study.

Alice Jones is a new interviewer, working on her first study. Her performance shows some serious weaknesses. She either was not adequately trained or she is being somewhat overwhelmed by the interviewing situations, and requires rapid attention and help. The problems which manifest themselves in her work tend to be characteristic of new interviewers, but hers appear to be more serious than usual. It is likely that with additional training, her performance will show rapid and marked improvement. If it does not, she will have to be dropped from the staff. Copies of the coding sheets were provided on which problems were circled in red. She was also referred to her *Interviewer's Manual* to help her to recognize the principles underlying the issues being raised. This feedback is designed to correct all three of the situations which produce poor performances (page 33); it provides:

1. Identification and analysis of specific examples of poor performance (tapes and coding sheets).

2. Means to understanding the principles being violated by consulting appropriate sections of an *Interviewer's Manual.*

3. Recognition of the need to acquire greater skill; for example, an interviewer might be asked to examine his poor probes and then to reword them effectively.

This material also provides a sound basis with which the interviewer and supervisor can formulate goals for improvement, and training can be focused directly upon instances in which the interviewer performed inadequately. During the training, the interviewer should record several more sessions for practice only, and together she and the supervisor should code the tapes while the supervisor provides feedback.

<hr/>

[1] The Survey Research Center of the Institute for Social Research (The University of Michigan) publishes an interviewer's manual which contains information on interviewing techniques. This is available for purchase from the SRC Publishing Division.

INTERVIEWER TRAINING AND SUPERVISION

Table 5-1

Report to Interviewers on Analysis of Recorded Interviews

NAME OF INTERVIEWER: _MARY SMITH_   Date: _Nov. 1974_

This report is based on interviews numbered _042_, _123_, _132_, _142_, _201_, taken on Study number _764_ .

Table A
PERCENTAGE OF INTERVIEWER ACTIVITIES

Activity	Average all Interviewers	Average for your Interviews	Range of your Interviews	Your previous Average
Question asking	78.7	86.8	68.5-97.4	74.3
Probing	17.9	11.3	2.1- 27.8	22.9
Other	2.1	.8	0 - 2.8	1.5
Q. skips	1.3	1.1	0 - 5.9	1.3
TOTAL*				100 %

*Inaudible portions of tape and other unclear activity is omitted from this analysis.

OVERALL RATINGS:

A. Pace of interviews   [Much too fast] [(Somewhat too fast)] [About right] [Somewhat too slow] [Much too slow]

Especially at the beginning of interviews, you have a tendency to read the questions too fast and not pause after a response.

B. Voice inflection

In reading the list in Q42 you had a tendency to drop your voice on each item. Should be asked as question.

NOTES:

This analysis shows you are doing much better in asking questions as worded. You are probing less than before. The probes used are more often acceptable non-directive ones. Overall, this analysis shows improvement over previous performance. Good work!

You should watch your speed in question-asking (see your Interviewers' Manual.)

Table 5-2

PERCENTAGE OF EACH TYPE OF ACTIVITY WHICH WAS ACCEPTABLE AND UNACCEPTABLE

Activity	Average for all Interviewers	Average for your Interviews	Range of your Interviews	Your previous Average
Question asking:				
Codes 11	84.8	93.3	82.8- 99.1	
12	9.7	5.4	0.5- 13.3	
% acceptable	94.5	98.7	96.1- 100	78.2
Codes 21	0.0	0.0	0-0	
22	5.4	1.3	0- 3.9	
23	0.1	0.0	0-0	
% unacceptable	5.5	1.3	0- 3.9	21.8
Probing:				
Codes 31	19.0	25.6	0- 93.3	
32	41.5	34.8	0- 47.9	
33	0.0	0.0	0-0	
34	18.7	20.4	0- 21.7	
35	10.7	9.6	0- 10.0	
% acceptable	89.9	90.4	75- 100	80.1
Codes 41	2.2	2.6	0- 14.3	
42	5.9	3.0	0- 7.4	
43	0.0	0.0	0-0	
45	1.8	3.9	0- 8.5	
% unacceptable	11.1	9.6	0- 25.0	19.9
Other:				
Codes 51	19.4	7.1	0- 14.2	
57	0.0	0.0	0-0	
58	28.7	42.9	0- 100.0	
% acceptable	48.1	50.0	0- 100.0	47.3
Codes 62	14.0	7.1	0- 14.2	
63	22.1	35.8	0- 43.8	
67	0.0	0.0	0-0	
68	15.8	7.1	0- 14.2	
% unacceptable	51.9	50.0	0- 100.0	52.7
Other (skips):				
Code 71	90.5	93.2		
% acceptable	90.5	93.2		92.5
Codes 72	6.7	5.6		
73	2.8	1.2		
75	0.0	0.0		
78	0.0	0.0		
% unacceptable	9.5	6.8		7.5

INTERVIEWER TRAINING AND SUPERVISION

Table 5-3

Report to Interviewers on Analysis of Recorded Interviews

NAME OF INTERVIEWER: _ALICE JONES_   Date: _Nov 1974_

This report is based on interviews numbered _004_, _005_, _009_, _016_, _023_, taken on Study number _764_.

Table A
PERCENTAGE OF INTERVIEWER ACTIVITIES

Activity	Average all Interviewers	Average for your Interviews	Range of your Interviews	Your previous Average
Question asking	78.7	85.6	64.0-93.5	
Probing	17.9	9.1	5.3-14.6	_None_
Other	2.1	1.3	0-1.9	
Q. skips	1.3	4.0	1.4-5.2	
TOTAL*	100%	100%		100%

*Inaudible portions of tape and other unclear activity is omitted from this analysis.

OVERALL RATINGS:

A. Pace of interviews | Much too fast | Somewhat too fast | About right | Somewhat too slow | Much too slow |

B. Voice inflection _Good reading of questions. You sound natural and interested when asking questions. Good. At times a slight tendency not to emphasize important words._

NOTES: _At times you do not probe enough to obtain adequate responses. Your probes also tend to be directive. Please review the manual and be sure you are familiar with each question's objectives. You skipped some questions. This means that you need to study the question-naire to learn the skip patterns. These are your first interviews and we send this analysis to help you in your training. Inter-viewing is a complex activity, so don't be discouraged — your per-formance is adequate for one who is just starting to work. Your supervisor will see you soon to help you work on these problems. Good luck._

I am returning interviews 005 + 016 (both the tapes + the q'aires) and the copies of the coding sheets for these interviews. Please listen to the tapes and follow along with the coding sheets. When you come to an unacceptable probe (marked in red) codes in 40's, stop the machine and be sure you know why the code is unacceptable. Think what you would do to make it acceptable. And listen for responses which should have been probed.

38

Table 5-4

PERCENTAGE OF EACH TYPE OF ACTIVITY WHICH WAS ACCEPTABLE AND UNACCEPTABLE

Activity	Average for all Interviewers	Average for your Interviews	Range of your Interviews	Your previous Average
Question asking:				
Codes 11	84.7	79.5		*NONE*
12	9.7	11.2		
% acceptable	94.5	90.7		
Codes 21	0.0	0.0		
22	5.4	8.4		
23	0.1	0.9		
% unacceptable	5.5	9.3		
Probing:				
Codes 31	19.0	16.5		
32	41.5	33.2		
33	0.0	0.0		
34	18.7	16.4		
35	10.7	11.3		
% acceptable	89.9	77.4		
Codes 41	2.2	4.5		
42	5.9	9.3		
43	0.0	0.0		
45	1.8	8.8		
% unacceptable	11.1	22.6		
Other:				
Codes 51	19.4	18.5		
57	0.0	0.0		
58	28.7	27.5		
% acceptable	48.1	46.0		
Codes 62	14.0	18.3		
63	22.1	16.2		
67	0.0	0.0		
68	15.8	19.5		
% unacceptable	51.9	54.0		
Other (skips):				
Code 71	90.5	90.0		
% acceptable	90.5	90.0		
Codes 72	6.7	9.2		
73	2.8	0.8		
75	0.0	0.0		
78	0.0	0.0		
% unacceptable	9.5	10.0		

CHAPTER 6

OTHER USES OF THE BEHAVIOR DATA

The interviewer behavior data can also be used for applications other than the evaluation of interviewer performances. Some applications use the data in the form in which they are fed back to interviewers; others require some modifications in the coding system itself.

ASSESSMENT OF INTERVIEWER TRAINING METHODS

The behavior codes provide a basis for evaluating the training methods which were used with the interviewer. A cumulative summary of all of the coded interviews conducted by all of the interviewers in the program can be examined for general weaknesses. A high rate of unacceptable techniques indicates that there was probably some deficiency in the training program. By examining the codes, one can develop hypotheses as to the nature of the difficulty.

EVALUATING OVERALL INTERVIEWER STAFF PERFORMANCE

It is useful to generalize about all interviewers' performances so that average proportions and percentages of behavior can be calculated, and the researcher can determine the degree to which systematic interviewing techniques were used in conducting his survey. The authors of an interview schedule may also find the total code frequencies and proportions for each question in the schedule useful. For instance, a question that is consistently read incorrectly should probably be reworded for future use. As was mentioned earlier, the behavior data which are averaged for all interviewers can also be a valuable aid in feeding back performance data to an individual interviewer. The points of comparison which they provide often encourage goal-setting by the interviewer.

CODING OTHER TYPES OF INTERVIEWS

While the behavior code was originally developed for use with interviews which are conducted with specific schedules of questions in a survey research setting, it has considerable potential for use in other kinds of interviews. Many of the behaviors which occur in journalistic, legal, and medical interviews are basically the same as those which occur in a social research interview. Modifications in the code categories could be made to incorporate different question types, especially when there are rules of acceptability, as in legal examinations.

People who are being trained to conduct these kinds of interviews could receive coded data from tapes of practice interviews and role-playing situations. The data would indicate those areas in which further training and practice might be necessary.

The flexibility and adaptability of the coding scheme will permit even more varied uses for it in the future, but the coders must always be trained thoroughly in accordance with the adapted scheme, and an effort should always be made to prove the reliability of whatever coding is done.

COMPARISON BETWEEN CONTENT CODES FROM TAPES AND THOSE FROM INTERVIEW PROTOCOLS

This comparison requires that the taped interview be coded according to standards which are different from those for behavior coding. One can code the content of the interview from the tapes, using the same code which is used for the regular written interviews. By comparing the codes for the same interview from two independent coding procedures, one can check on the accuracy and completeness of the interviewer's note-taking and reporting procedures.

CHAPTER 7

MANUAL FOR USING THE BEHAVIOR CODE

The first two sets of codes cover the general area of question-asking behavior. In the two-digit system, these are codes in the 10's and 20's, and are the only codes which may not be repeated on a question. A question will have either a code from the 10's or a code from the 20's. The following provides a brief description of the category for each code, followed by clarification and examples.

Category 10—Question Asked Correctly

The first set of codes, those in the 10's, cover those instances in which the interviewer asks the question correctly.

Code

11   *11: Asks question and choices exactly as printed on questionnaire.*

Example:

Question as printed on questionnaire	Question as read by interviewer
Do you have a college degree?	I: Do you have a college degree? (Code: 11)

Contractions such as "weren't" for "were not" are coded as correct. If it becomes necessary to paraphrase parenthetical expressions which refer to the persons included in the question, the reading should still be coded 11 as long as the paraphrase includes all of those people who should be mentioned.

Example:

We would like to know about your (Head's) present job; are you (Head) working now, looking for work, retired, or what?	(If the wife of the Head of the Household is being interviewed, then the question should be paraphrased to:)

I: We would like to know about your "husband's" present job; is "he" working now, looking for work, retired, or what?

(11)

Code 11 should also be used if the interviewer supplies conjunctions such as "and," "or," and "well" either as transition remarks or as prefaces to questions.

Example:

Is there anything about your health that either gives you trouble with or makes it hard for you to do things you feel you should do, with your family or around the house?	I: Is there anything about your health that either gives you trouble with or makes it hard for you to do things you feel you should do, with your family or around the house?

(11)

R: Yes, there is.

How much trouble does this give you, a lot, some, or very little?	I: "And" how much trouble does this give you, a lot, some, or very little?

(11)

Code 11 should not be used either when a question which has already been asked is repeated or when a question which should be omitted is asked; there are separate codes for these behaviors (see 32 and 27).

12   *12: Asks question with slight change which does not alter frame of reference, and the question choices are read exactly as printed on the questionnaire.*

If the reading of the printed question is modified, but still essentially correct, with only *unimportant* or *repetitious* words dropped, then the reading should be coded 12. However, if *key words* or concepts which may affect the meaning of the question are either added, omitted, or changed, code 12 should not be used. Meaningless space-fillers such as, "Now I'd like to ask you . . ." or "The next question is . . ." which neither change the meaning nor clarify a question should be coded 12.

MANUAL FOR USING THE BEHAVIOR CODE

Example:

Question as printed on questionnaire	Question as read by interviewer
Have you gone to school in the past year?	I: "The next question is," have you gone to school in the past year? (12)

Unimportant words may be omitted.

Example:

Is there anything which you have cut down on or do not do because you think that doing it would be bad for your health?	I: Is there anything which you have cut down on or do not do because you think doing it would be bad for your health? (12)

Unimportant words may be added.

Example:

How satisfied are you with the moral standards in your community; the way in which people behave?	I: How satisfied are you with the moral standards in your community, "that is," the way in which people behave. (12)

If the introduction to a set of questions is modified, each question in that set should be coded 12 because the introduction relates to and influences each question in the set.

Example:

Here are several different things people say they have done to call attention to a problem or get something done.	I: Here are things people say they have done to call attention to a problem or to get something done.
(a) Have you ever gone on a march?	(a) Have you ever gone on a march? (12)
(b) Signed a petition about some issue?	R: No
(c) Picketed an agency or organization?	I: Signed a petition about some issue? (12)
	R: No
	I: Picketed an agency or organization? (12)

Category 20—Question Asked Incorrectly

The code categories in the 20's cover those situations in which the interviewer asks the question incorrectly.

Code

21   *21: Asks stem of question as printed but does not ask choices as printed.*

Example:

Question as printed on questionnaire	Question as read by interviewer
Now let's talk about things that may give a person a feeling of satisfaction. Would you tell me if you are very satisfied, satisfied, dissatisfied or very dissatisfied with the kind of neighborhood you live in?	I: Now let's talk about things that may give a person a feeling of satisfaction. Would you tell me if you are "satisfied or dissatisfied" with the kind of neighborhood you live in? (21)
How much did all your utilities such as heat and electricity cost you last year; was it less than $100, $100-200, $200-300, $300-400, or what?	I: How much did all your utilities such as heat and electricity cost you last year; was it less than $100, $100-200, or what? (21)

22   *22: Asks question incorrectly in a significantly altered manner.*

Code 22 should be used for any alteration which changes the meaning of the question, or if only part of the question is asked.

Example:

Question as printed on questionnaire	Question as read by interviewer
What (is/was) your main occupation; that is, what sort of work do you do?	I: What is your main occupation? (22)
Compared with five years ago, are you and your family able to buy more and better things than you did then, are you having to cut back on what you buy, or are you living the same as you did then?	I: Compared with five years ago, are you and your family able to buy more and better things than you did then, or are you having to cut back on what you buy? (22)

48

Code 22 should be used if a key word or concept is either added, omitted, or changed, even if this does not alter the frame of reference. Code 22 should also be used if key words are added.

Example:

How much do you earn?   I: *"About"* how much do you earn?   (22)

Code 22 is used if a key word is omitted.

Example:

Did you or anyone else here attend any parent-teacher meetings in the last year?	I: Did you or anyone else here attend parent-teacher meetings in the last year? (22)
Have you had a cold or the flu in the past month?	I: Have you had a cold in the past month? (22)

Code 22 is used if a key word is changed.

Example:

Should parents organize public marches?	I: Should parents organize public demonstrations? (22)
Are there jobs around here that just aren't worth taking?	I: Are there jobs around here that just aren't worth it? (22)

Code 22 should be used if enough insignificant changes have been made to confuse the meaning.

Example:

For a person like yourself, what are some of the advantages of the small foreign cars over the new small American cars?	I: For a person like you, what are some advantages of a small foreign car over a new small American car? (22)

Code 22 should be used when the respondent interrupts the interviewer by responding to a question before the interviewer has completed it, and the interviewer does not then complete the question. If the interviewer does complete the question, exactly as it is written, despite the interruption, the reading should be coded 11.

If the introduction to a set of questions is read incorrectly, each question in that set should be coded 22.

Example:

Here are several steps that some people feel could help solve the problem of race tensions. Would you favor:	I: Here are several steps that could help solve the problem of race tensions: Would you favor investigating to see if there is racism in the local schools? (22)
(a) Investigating to see if there is racism in the local schools?	R: Yes
(b) Government job training programs for blacks?	I: Government job training programs for blacks? (22)
	R: Yes

If any or all of the question is read incorrectly and the interviewer immediately corrects himself with no interruption or intervening behavior (by either interviewer or respondent) the first incorrect question should be ignored, and the reading should be coded 11 or 12, whichever is appropriate.

Example:

When was your last visit to a doctor?	I: When is your, excuse me, when was your last visit to a doctor? (11)

23   *23: Does not ask question as printed, but assumes answer to a question by making a statement.*

Example:

Question as printed on questionnaire	Question as read by interviewer
Do you own this (home/apartment), pay rent, or what?	I: And you rent this apartment. (23)

Code 23 should be used only if some verbal statement replaces a printed question; if there is no verbal behavior, code 71 or 72 should be used, or when appropriate, code 73 (see 70's).

27 *27: Asks question which should have been skipped.*

Example:

Question as printed on questionnaire	Question as read by interviewer

2. Are you over 17 years old?   I: Are you over 17 years old?

(11)

| Yes | | No | ▶ Go to Q4   R: No

3. Are you registered to vote?   I: Are you registered to vote?

(27)

| Yes | | No | R: No

The second two sets of codes cover general probing behavior. In the two-digit system, these are codes in the 30's and 40's. The behaviors which these categories include are those queries, statements, and confirmations made by interviewers which are designed to encourage the respondent either to respond or to enlarge upon or clarify what he has already said.

Category 30—Correct Probe Used

The codes in the 30's are for non-directive probes. To be non-directive, a probe must effect no limitation or change in the frame of reference of the question; the frame of reference of the response should not be limited or changed either.

Code

31 *31: Makes up non-directive probe.*

Example:

I: Anything else?
   What do you mean?
   What particularly?
   What was that?
   Would you tell me more about
      that?
   Why do you say that?
   Pardon me?
   Could you repeat that?   (31)

32   *32: Repeats question or part of question correctly.*

Example:

Question as printed on questionnaire	Question as read by interviewer

If you were to get enough money to live as comfortably as you'd like for the rest of your life, would you continue to work?

I: (Reads Q. OK)   (11)

R: I love my work.

I: (Reads entire Q again)   (32)

What do you see as the most important problems we have in this country?

I: What do you see as the most important problems we have in this country?   (11)

R: There are so many . . . uh . . .

I: Well, what comes to mind when I say the most important problems?   (32)

Code 32 should be used if the question is repeated correctly, even if it was asked incorrectly the first time.

Example:

Is there public transportation within walking distance of here?

I: Is there public transportation here?   (22)

R: Well, there's the bus . . .

I: Is that within walking distance of here?   (32)

If a question has a wide range of response categories and a respondent's previous answer implies a particular area of the categories available, then the interviewer may repeat only those categories in that general area and still be coded 32.

Example:

Would you tell me if you are very satisfied, satisfied, dissatisfied, or very dissatisfied with your present housing?

I: Would you tell me if you are very satisfied, satisfied, dissatisfied, or very dissatisfied with your present housing?   (11)

R: Oh, I'm satisfied.

I: Would you say very satisfied or satisfied? (32)

34   *34: Repeats the respondent's response, or part of it, correctly.*

Example:

R: I think things have changed
for the worse.

I: For the worse. (34)

Code 34 should be used for a correct summary of the respondent's response.

Example:

Question as printed on questionnaire	Question as read by interviewer
Would you say it's very true, somewhat true, or not at all true that the police don't treat people with respect?	I: Would you say it's very true, somewhat true, or not at all true that the police don't treat people with respect? (11)
	R: Oh, I think they always treat people with respect.
	I: So that's not true. (34)

Code 34 should be used if the interviewer repeats part of the question or response in order to choose a correct response category.

Example:

Compared with last year, are you able to buy more and better things now, are you having to cut back on what you buy, or are you living the same as you did then?	I: (Reads Q. OK) (11)
	R: No, I think the first one.
	I: Buying more. (34)
	R: Umm-hmm.

Buying more   Cutting back

Living the same   DK

In these cases, code 34 should be used rather than code 32.

35   *35: Confirms a frame of reference for respondent.*

Example: R: Did you say 'freedom'?

                                        I: Yes   (35)

                            R: Does the money I make
                                  as a cab driver count?

                            I: Yes   (35)

Code 35 should be used if the interviewer provides a correct clarification in response to a request for one.

Example:

                            R: What do you mean by
                                  neighborhood?

                            I: Whatever 'neighborhood'
                                  means to you.   (35)

Code 35 should be used if the respondent requests a clarification and the interviewer reads an adequate part of the question in response. If the interviewer reads the entire question after a request, code 32 should be used rather than code 35.

Example:

Question as printed on questionnaire	Question as read by interviewer
As to the economic policy of the government—I mean steps taken to fight inflation or unemployment—would you say that government is doing a good job, only fair, or a poor job?	I: As to the economic policy of the government--I mean steps taken to fight inflation or unemployment--would you say the government is doing a good job, only fair, or a poor job? (11)
	R: You mean like the wage price freeze?
	I: I mean steps taken to fight inflation or unemployment. (35)

Example:

How much are you *personally* **affected by air pollution—very much, a little, or not at all?**	I: How much are you personally affected by air pollution —very much, a little, or not at all? (11)
	R: You mean is smog a problem?
	I: I mean how much are *you* *personally* affected by air pollution—very much, a little, or not at all. (32)

Category 40—Inappropriate Probe Used

The codes in the 40's cover those instances in which the interviewer uses directive probes which are not printed on the questionnaire. A probe is directive if it either changes or limits the frame of reference of the question or limits the response possibilities.

Code

41   *41: Makes up probe which is directive.*

Example:

I: That's all?
Nothing else?   (41)

A probe is also directive if it suggests possible answers to the respondent either directly or by providing information in addition to that which the respondent and the original question have already given.

Example:

Question as printed on questionnaire	Question as read by interviewer

Example:

Have you had any health problems in the last week?	I: Have you had any health problems in the last week? (11)
	R: What do you mean by health problems?
	I: Things like colds and flu. (41)

42   *42: Repeats question and/or choices incorrectly* **or** *gives incorrect summary or statement of respondent's response.*

Example:

Question as printed on questionnaire	Question as read by interviewer
About how much rent do you pay a month?	I: About how much rent do you pay a month? (11)
	R: Oh, between $100 and $150.
	I: So you'd say about $125? (42)
How likely is it that you could find a job; is it very likely, somewhat likely, or not very likely?	I: How likely is it that you could find a job; is it very likely, somewhat likely or not very likely? (11)
	R: Oh, it's possible.
	I: Would you say it's very likely, then? (42)

If a respondent interrupts the interviewer while he is using the response choices as a probe, then code 32 should be used. If the interviewer does not offer all of the choices when no general area has been indicated by the respondent's previous answer, then code 42 should be used.

43   *43: Gives an introduction which is directive.*

Code 43 should be used if the interviewer rewords an introduction from the questionnaire in a directive manner.

Example:

Question as printed on questionnaire	Question as read by interviewer
I'd like to ask you some questions about health matters.	I: I'd like to ask you some questions about how you think your health is. (43)

Code 43 should be used if the interviewer makes up his own introduction to a section which is directive.

Example:

(Questions concerning employment are next.)	I: Now we'd like to know how much you like your job . . . (43)

45   *45: Interprets question.*

Example:

Question as printed on questionnaire	Question as read by interviewer
As you see it, is the idea that "We need tax reforms to make taxes fair for everyone," one which rich people support *more* **than you do or do they give it less support?**	I: As you see it, is the idea that "we need tax reforms to make taxes fair for everyone," one which rich people support more than you do or do they give it less support? That is, do rich folks want tax reforms as much as the rest of us? (11, 45)

Code 45 should be used if the interviewer volunteers a clarification in own words, whether or not it appears to be correct.

Example:

Are you making as much money now as you were a year ago, or more, or less?	I: Are you making as much money now as you were a year ago, or more, or less; that is, has your income changed? (11, 45)
During the next year, or so, do you think the government will be successful in reducing inflation, or do you expect that there will be little or no improvement?	I: During the next year or so, do you think the government will be successful in reducing inflation, or do you expect that there will be little or no improvement, that is, that the economy will keep on expanding? (11, 45)

Code 45 should be used if the interviewer gives an incorrect clarification.

Example:

How satisfied or dissatisfied are you with this neighborhood as a place to live?	I: How satisfied or dissatisfied are you with this neighborhood as a place to live? (11)
	R: What do you mean by neighborhood?
	I: Oh, this square mile. (45)

Code 45 should be used if the interviewer incorrectly confirms a frame of reference.

Example:

Is your standard of living higher, the same, or lower than that of your neighbors?	I: Is your standard of living higher, the same, or lower than that of your neighbors? (11)
	R: You mean is my house better?
	I: Yes (45)

The next two sets of codes are intended for various behaviors which may occur during an interview, which are not directly associated either with asking questions or probing for more information, but which affect the interviewer-respondent interaction. In the two-digit system, these codes are the 50's and 60's. The behaviors which these codes represent may generally be categorized as behaviors which could in some way affect the validity of the information being gathered: remarks designed to build rapport, evaluative remarks, interruptions, incomplete or inaccurate recording of a respondent's answers, etc.

Category 50—Appropriate Behavior

The codes in the 50's represent those behaviors which conform to the present principles of interviewing technique, that is, they represent behaviors which either increase or at least do not jeopardize the validity of the information being gathered.

Code

51   *51: Helps respondent to understand his role and what the study wants; gives task-oriented clarification about respondent's job.*

Example:

> I: We are interested in your
> opinions.
> There are no right or wrong
> answers; we just want to
> know how you feel.
> Please use the card in choos-
> ing your answer.
> We've already touched on this
> subject, but let me ask you
> about this . . .
> This survey is interested in
> how people all over the
> country feel about certain
> health issues.   (51)

58 *58: Makes other acceptable remarks or exhibits other acceptable behavior.*

Code 58 should be used if a remark is neutral.

Example:

> I: Do you want to stop to get
> the boys' lunch?
> Maybe you could do that
> when we're through.
> Just let me know if you want
> to stop for a while.   (58)

Code 58 should be used for statements which reinforce current behavior.

Example:

> I: It's OK if you want to take
> time to think about the rest
> of these.   (58)

As a general rule, a brief "OK," "Fine," etc. is coded as feedback. Non-words such as m-m-m, or uh-h-h are not coded.

Category 60—Inappropriate or Evaluative Remarks or Behavior

The codes in the 60's cover those remarks or behaviors which are either considered inappropriate or which in some way may decrease or jeopardize the validity of the information being gathered.

<u>Code</u>

62   *62: Interrupts the respondent.*

Example:

Question as printed on questionnaire	Question as read by interviewer
Over the next six months, which do you think will go up more, prices or wages?	I: Over the next six months, which do you think will go up more, prices or wages? (11)
	R: Gee, I don't know much about . . . uh . . . that, I guess I'd have to . . .
	I: Which do you think will go up more? (62, 32)

63   *63: Gives personal opinion or evaluation.*

Code 63 should be used for any indication of either agreement or disagreement with the respondent.

Example:

Question as printed on questionnaire	Question as read by interviewer
Do you or anyone else in the family here own a car or truck?	I: Do you or anyone else in the family here own a car or truck? (11)
	R: No.
	I: But I saw a car in your garage! (63)
	R: I think taxes are too high.
	I: Boy, I'm with you! (63)

Code 63 should be used for a personal opinion.

Example:	I: This neighborhood is really well kept. (63)

Code 63 should be used for any praise or criticism of the respondent.

Example:

> I: I think it's just wonderful
> the way you've overcome
> this adversity and succeeded
> so well. (63)

Code 63 should be used for unacceptable feedback.

Example:

> I: Don't go so fast; I can't get
> it all down.
>
> But you said no a minute
> ago. (63)

Code 63 should be used for expressions of surprise or displeasure.

Example:

> I: You don't mind going to
> the dentist! (63)

67   Optional

67: Records response either incorrectly or incompletely on questionnaire.

Code 67 should be considered a special code for separate studies or occasional use only, because it distracts the coder from the verbal behavior.

Code 67 can only be used if the coder has the questionnaire for that particular interview available as he codes.

Example:

> R: I go to the grocery store once
> every two weeks.
>
> I: (records) I go to the grocery
> once a week. (67)
>
> R: Two or three times a week.
>
> I: (records) Three times per
> week. (67)

68   *68: Makes other unacceptable remarks or exhibits other unacceptable behavior.*

Code 68 should be used when the interviewer reads his own instructions aloud.

Example:

I: Now I have to go to page 10.

You're unemployed, so I don't ask you these questions.　　(68)

Category 70—Non-recorded Behavior

This set of codes covers non-recorded or inaudible behavior, cases in which questions are not asked, there is no sound on the tape, etc. In the two-digit system, these codes are in the 70's.

Code

71　　*71: Skips question correctly.*

Code 71 should be used if a question is not read because of a skip pattern.

72　　*72: Omits question incorrectly.*

Code 72 should be used if a question is skipped when it should have been read. If there was *any* verbal behavior, then code 23 should be used.

73　　*73: Writes in previously obtained answer, no verbal behavior.*

Code 73 should be used when the interviewer does not ask a question because the respondent has just supplied the necessary information to answer it.

Code 73 should only be used when there is no verbal behavior on a question. If there is behavior, use code 23 or any other code which is appropriate. If there is any doubt about whether the respondent has supplied an answer to the question, use code 72 rather than 73.

75　　**Optional**

75: Fails to probe after inadequate answer.

Code 75 is listed here as optional because of the difficulties involved in using it. The coder must have a sophisticated level of understanding of the question's objective in order to determine when an answer is inadequate. This requires extensive coder training. In addition, in order to use this code the coder must both concentrate on coding the behavior which is occurring, and remain alert for behavior omissions. This is a difficult task.

Code 75 should be used when the respondent has given a response which does not meet the objectives of the question, and the interviewer fails to probe for additional information.

Example:

Question as printed on questionnaire	Question as read by interviewer
Do you remember when you were growing up whether your father was very much interested in politics, somewhat interested, or didn't he pay much attention?	I: Do you remember when you were growing up whether your father was very much interested in politics, somewhat interested, or didn't he pay much attention? (11)
	R: Oh, he was interested in Roosevelt. (75)
Did he think of himself mostly as a *Democrat*, as a *Republican*, as an *Independent*, or what?	I: Did he think of himself mostly as a *Democrat*, as a *Republican*, as an *Independent*, or what? (11)
	R: Oh, he was a Republican.

78   *78: Missing data, unknown.*

Code 78 should be used either if there is no sound on the tape or if the sound is unintelligible.

Category 80—Pace

The next set of codes is designed to provide information about the pace at which the interview was conducted and the voice inflection which was used. In the two-digit system, these codes are in the 80's. There are no clear-cut occasions for which these codes should be assigned. It is possible either to give an overall pace code for the entire interview or to code the pace at various selected spots in the interview, e.g., at the end of sections of questions. In order to determine the speed of delivery, the coder must measure the time which the interviewer takes just to ask the question, then divide this time by the number of words in that question. It is best to obtain an average speed using several questions of different lengths.

Code

81   *81: Reads questions more slowly than two words per second.*

82   *82: Reads questions at about two words per second.*

83   *83: Reads questions more quickly than two words per second.*

84   *84: Pace of entire interview seemed too slow for the respondent.*

Code 84 should be used if there were long silences after the respondent had completed his response.

85   *85: Pace of entire interview seemed about right for the respondent.*

Code 85 should be used if the interview was neither too slow, as defined for code 84, nor too fast, as defined for code 86.

86   *86: Pace of entire interview seemed too fast for the respondent.*

Code 86 should be used either if the interviewer began to ask the next question while the respondent was delivering pertinent information concerning the current question without digressing, or if the interviewer did not give the respondent enough time to think about his responses.

Code 86 should be used either if the interviewer probed more than once without waiting for the respondent's reply to each probe, or if the interviewer asked questions too rapidly for the respondent to comprehend them.

Voice Inflection

87   *87: Questions read in a wooden, expressionless manner. Interviewer is clearly "reading" rather than speaking naturally.*

88   *88: Questions asked with a rising inflection at the end.*

89   *89: Questions asked with voice dropped, so that they sound like statements instead of questions.*

If questions with lists are included, this code may be used specifically for the list as well as for the whole question.

Codes 87 through 89 should be used only once at the end of an interview; the coder should choose the one which best describes the entire interview.

Category 90—Background

The next set of codes covers those instances in which the interviewer provides any kind of background information. In the two-digit system, these codes are in the 90's.

It is not uncommon for many of the behaviors which this set of codes covers to occur before the interviewer actually begins to tape the interview, since many interviewers set up the tape recorder only after the respondent has agreed to the interview, following an introduction by the interviewer. Nevertheless, these behaviors do sometimes occur during the taped interview, and coding categories have been defined for them.

Code

91 *91: Mentions own name.*

Example:

E

I: Hello, I'm Mary Jones from the Survey Research Center of the University of Michigan.

(91)

92 *92: Mentions sponsorship.*

Example:

I: This study is being sponsored by a department of the University of Michigan. (92)

93 *93: Mentions anonymity.*

Example:

I: Everything you say will be confidential

Your name and address will never be identified in any way with the answers you give. (93)

94 *94: Mentions respondent selection.*

Example:

I: You were chosen quite impersonally as a particular person at this particular address.

(94)

I: When we combine interviews from people at all of these addresses, we will have a cross section of the area which we cover.

In order to keep our sample representative, I must use special procedures to select the person whom I interview. In this case, I must talk to your daughter rather than to you. (94)

95 *95: Mentions purpose of study.*

Example: I: This study is interested in finding out how people need and use public service programs such as health care, rehabilitation, income maintenance, and so on. (95)

Additional Notes

Uncoded Behavior

There are certain interviewer behaviors which should deliberately be left uncoded. For instance, comments such as, "Here's a blue card" are not coded, because interviewers who use gestures would be penalized. Also, if an introduction to either a question or a section is optional, it should not be coded unless the content of the interviewer's statement is inappropriate. Brief introductions such as, "The next question is . . . ," should not be coded. If the introduction is inappropriate or directive, it should be coded 43. Any conversation which occurs between the interviewer and a third person in the room should not be coded.

Brief repetitions should be coded only once.

Example:

R: Oh, you mean what I made if they hadn't taken my taxes out?

I: Yes, Yes.

(35) *once*

MANUAL FOR USING THE BEHAVIOR CODE

Code Summary

Code

11	Exact Question—no changes
12	Modified Question—slight changes which do not alter frame of reference
21	Stem Correct—errors in reading choices
22	Incorrect Question—reads only part of question, changes key words
23	Assumes Answer—does not read question, makes statement about answer
27	Inappropriate Question—asks question which should have been skipped
31	Invents Non-directive Probes—probes non-directively using own words
32	Repeats Question Correctly—repeats all or part of question correctly
34	Repeats Responses Correctly—repeats or summarizes R's response correctly
35	Correct Clarification—gives non-directive clarification when requested
41	Invents Directive Probe—probes directively using own words
42	Repeats Question or Response Incorrectly—repeats question or part incorrectly or R's response incorrectly
43	Directive Introduction—rewords an introduction in a directive manner
45	Interprets Question—gives incorrect clarification or interprets question
51	Helps R Understand Role—gives task-oriented information about R's role
58	Other Acceptable Remarks—makes other, more general, acceptable remarks
62	Interrupts Respondent—interrupts the respondent while he is talking
63	Personal Opinion—gives a personal opinion, agrees or disagrees
67	Records Incorrectly—writes down response incorrectly
68	Other Unacceptable Remarks—makes other inappropriate remarks
71	Correct Skip—skips a question correctly due to a skip pattern
72	Incorrect Omit—omits a question which should have been read
73	Previously Obtained Answer—writes in answer respondent has already given with no verbal exchange
75	Fails to Probe—fails to probe when answer is inadequate
78	Missing Data—no sound on tape
81	Slow Question Pace
82	Correct Question Pace
83	Fast Question Pace

84 Slow Interview Pace

85 Correct Interview Pace

86 Fast Interview Pace

87 Wooden Questions

88 Inflected Questions

89 Dropped Questions

91 Mentions Name

92 Mentions Sponsorship

93 Mentions Anonymity

94 Mentions Respondent Selection

95 Mentions Study Purpose

CHAPTER 8

SAMPLE CODED INTERVIEW

I. Sample Transcript of Tape Recorded Interview

Question as printed on questionnaire	Actual Interview*
1. **Our first question is about your present health in general. Within the last month, that is, since _____, have you had any sicknesses, illnesses, or any other problems with your health?**	I: Our first question is about your present health in general. Within the last month, that is since May 15, have you had any sicknesses, illnesses, injuries, or any other problems with your health? (11)
	R: Oh, really nothing worth, nothing worth mentioning, I guess.
	I: Nothing worth mentioning? (34)
	R: Well, I had, I had a little flu, ah, three weeks ago, that bothered me for a day or two, and, uh, what was it you wanted, sicknesses within the last month?
	I: Sicknesses, illnesses, injuries, or any other problems with your health, within the last month. (35)
	R: Well, I also hurt my arm. I was working down in the basement, lifting a box of heavy stuff, and it slipped and I strained my elbow and shoulder some.
	I: Mm-hmm. (No code--not a word)

---

*Assigned code appears in parentheses.

69

R: That's all, in the last month.

(pause)

1a. **Please tell me something (more) about health problems you have had during the month.**

I: Could you please tell me something more about health problems you have had during the last month? (12)

R: Well, I think that covers, covers everything that, uh, what did I say? Along with the flu I did have a headache, but that's all.

2. **Now we would like to ask you how you feel these days. In general, how is your health now? Would you say your health is excellent, very good, good, fair, or poor?**

I: All right. (58)
Now we would like to ask you how you feel these days. In general, how is your health now? Would you say your health is excellent, very good, good, fair, or poor? (11)

R: Oh, I think it's all right, now that I'm over the flu.

I: Would you say, then, it is excellent, very good, good, or fair? (32)

R: Oh, I'd say it's excellent.

3. **What kinds of problems do you have with your health? What's wrong with your health?**

I: Excellent. (34)
All right. (58)
What kinds of problems do you have with your health? What's wrong with your health? (11)

R: Oh, I don't really know of anything that's uh, that's wrong. I guess, uh, I have a little arthritis once in a while, um, and the doctor told me I had a slight tendency to have high blood pressure, but that's, that's all. Besides that, I'm in fine shape.

Now we would like to know how your health compares with others.

4. *What about physical fitness.* **Compared to (men/women) your own age, would you say you are much more physically fit, more, about**

I: Okay. Fine. (58)
Now we would like to know how your health compares with others. What about physical fitness? Compared to men and women your own

70

the same, less physically fit, or much less fit?

age, would you say you are much more physically fit, more, the same, less, or much less? (22)

R: Oh, I think I'm, I'm in better shape than, than uh, other men my own age.

I: Would you say much more, or more? (32)

R: Oh, I'd say more.

5. Now about *energy*. Compared to (men/women) your own age, would you say you have much more *energy*, more energy, about the same, less, or much less energy?

I: Now about energy. Compared to men your own age, would you say you have much more energy, more energy, about the same, less, or much less energy? (11)

R: Oh, I'd say about the same, I think.

6. What about *enjoying life*. Compared to (men/women) your own age, would you say you are enjoying life much more, more, about the same, less, or much less?

I: What about enjoying life? Compared to men your own age, would you say you are enjoying life much more, more, about the same, or less? (21)

R: Oh, I think about the same.

7.1. Here are some other health conditions you may have had any time *during the past year* even though they may not bother you now. Have you had any of the following conditions at any time during the last 12 months, that is, since (month) of 1972? Skin trouble?

I: Here are some other health conditions you may have had any time during the past year, even though they may not bother you now. Have you had any of the following conditions at any time during the last twelve months, that is, since June of 1972? Skin trouble? (11)

R: For how long a period did you say?

I: Any time during the past year, especially if it bothers you now. (45)

R: Past year. Uh, skin trouble, no.

7.2. Rheumatism or arthritis?

I: Rheumatism, or arthritis? (11)

R: Yes, I have a little arthritis.

7.3. Bronchitis?

I: Oh, that's right, you just
     mentioned that to me.   (58)
     Bronchitis?   (11)

R: No.

7.4. Sinus trouble?

I: Sinus trouble?   (11)

R: Well, I have a cold once in a while.
     I had a cold about six months ago,
     and I, I don't know, whether, uh,
     whether that's sinus or not.

7.5. Trouble getting to sleep?

I: All right. I'll make a note of
     that.   (58)
     Trouble getting to sleep?   (11)

R: (laughs) No.

7.6. Trouble with teeth?

I: (laughs) Okay.   (58)
     Trouble with teeth?   (11)

R: Nope.

7.7. Cold or flu?

I: Cold or, well you just mentioned
     you had a cold so that's yes.   (23)

R: I had a cold--it was about, uh, six
     months ago, but I'm not sure that
     I really get troubled by it, uh, I
     mean, I'm not troubled by colds.
     I have a cold once in a while.

I: That's fine.   (51)
     The question here just asks you
     if you've *had* any of these condi-
     tions during the last 12 months. (35)

R: (interrupting) Oh! Oh yes, I did.

7.8. Heart trouble?

I: Heart trouble?   (11)

R: No.

7.9. Allergy?

I: Allergy?   (11)

R: Mm, no . . .

8. Is there anything about the kind of work you do or the conditions you work in that you regard as dangerous or as bad for your health?

I: All right. (58)
Now we have to turn to another section. (58)
The next question is: Is there anything about the kind of work you do or the conditions you work in that you regard as dangerous or bad for your health? (11)

R: Well, there's only one, there's only one kind of a thing. See, I'm maintenance engineer in one of the buildings over here, and every once in a while we have to clean with, uh, with, uh, some chemicals, and I get a little worried about all the fumes those chemicals give off. That's about all.

8a. What is this (are these)?
8b. Would you say this is (these are) a serious or slight problem for you?

I: (71)
Would you say that this is a serious or slight problem for you? (11)

R: Oh, I think only a slight problem.

9. Think about the kind of activities which you usually do in your (work/housework/school work). Do you have enough strength and energy to do these things as well as you would like?

I: Mm-hmm. (58)
Think about the kind of activities which you usually do in your work. Do you have enough strength and energy to do these things as well as you would like? (11)

R: Enough strength and energy? . . .

I: Yes. (35)

R: Um, well, I suppose so.

10. What about five years in the future? Do you think you will have enough strength and energy to do your (work/housework) as well as you do it now?

I: All right. (58)
What about five years in the future? Do you think you will have enough strength and energy to do your work as well as you do it now? (11)

R: Oh, I think so. I expect to be as well five years from now as I am now.

11. **What about activities which you enjoy in your free time, such as the things you like to do either alone, with your family, or with friends? First, what are some of the free-time activities which you most enjoy doing?**

I: Fine. (58)
   What about activities which you enjoy in your free time, such as the things you like to do either alone, with your family, or with friends? First, what are some of the free-time activities which you most enjoy doing? (11)

R: Do you mean like sports?

I: Any free-time activities which you enjoy doing. (45)

R: Ah . . .

I: Excuse me, it says the free-time activities which you *most* enjoy doing. (32)

R: Well, I suppose in the, in the summer I like to play golf; in the winter I bowl. Those are the two things I think I enjoy most.

I: Golf and bowling? (34)

R: Right.

12. **Thinking about these activities which you enjoy, do you have enough strength and energy to do them as much and as well as you would like?**

I: Thinking about these activities which you enjoy, do you have enough strength and energy to do them as much, and as well as you would like? (11)

R: Well, I, I never bowl as good--and I don't really play golf like I'd like either. I'd like to do, I'd like to do much better at both of those.

I: Let me re-read the question for you. (58)
   Thinking about these activities which you enjoy, do you have enough strength and energy to do them as much and as well as you would like? (32)

R: Oh. Oh, yeah. The problem is not energy. I have plenty of energy, and I . . .

I: (INTERVIEWER INTERRUPTS) Then you would say yes to this question about having enough strength and energy? (62, 42)

R: Well, I guess I would, now that you put it like that.

13. Do you have enough strength and energy to do these free-time activities as much and as well as you did them (five/ten) years ago?

I: Do you have enough strength and energy to do these free-time activities as much and as well as you did them five years ago? (11)

R: Well, I, uh, I guess, I perhaps get a little more tired going around the golf course, but, uh, not really anything to amount to much.

I: Well, perhaps I could re-read this question, also. (58)
I'd like to have a "Yes" or "No" answer. (51)
Do you have enough strength and energy to do these free-time activities as much and as well as you did them five years ago? (32)

R: Not quite as well.

I: I'll make a note of that. (58)

14. Have you visited a doctor in the past month, that is, since _____?

I: Have you visited a doctor in the last month, that is, since May 15? (12)

R: Yes, about my shoulder. The doctor looked at it.

15. Have you been in a hospital in the last 12 months, that is, since _____?

I: Have you been in a hospital in the last 12 months, since June 15, 1972? (12)

R: Not, not since 5 years ago.

I: Not since 5 years ago? (34)

R: Yes.

16. Are you married, separated, divorced, widowed, or have you never been married?

I: Now, I have a few questions about you.
Are you married, separated, divorced, widowed . . . (22)

R: (interrupting) I'm married.

17. What is the highest grade of school, or year of college you completed?

I: You're married. (34)
All right. (58)
What is the highest grade of school or year of college you completed? (11)

R: Oh, I got through, ah, I got through high school.

17a. Did you get a high school graduation diploma or pass a high school equivalency test?

I: Did you get a high school graduation diploma, or pass a high school equivalency test? (11)

R: Yeah, I got a diploma.

17b. Do you have a college degree?

I: And, do you have a college degree? (11)

R: No.

18. To get an accurate picture of people's financial situation, we need to know the income of all the families we interview. Would you please tell me the letter on this card that indicates how much income *you and your family* received from all sources during last year, 1972; I mean before taxes or any deductions?

I: All right. (58)
To get an accurate picture of peoples' financial situation, we need to know the income of all the families we interview. Would you please tell me the letter on this card that indicates how much income you, and your family received from all sources during last year, 1972. I mean, before taxes, or any deductions. (11)

R: Oh, that's hard. I'm not sure as I can remember that very well.

I: Well, as best you can remember, which letter would you pick? (31)

SAMPLE CODED INTERVIEW

R: Oh, I suppose it would, it would
come, ah, in, E. It was around
10,000 dollars.

I: E.   (34)

Well, thank you very much.   (58)

R: You're welcome.

SAMPLE CODED INTERVIEW

II. Coding Sheet from Sample Interview

Project # _011120_   Interview # _037_   Interviewer # _12_
     (cols. 1-6)   (cols. 7-9)   (cols. 10-11)

(cols. 12–15) Q#	(cols. 16–80) Behavior Code							
1.0	11	34	35					
1.1	12	58						
2.0	11	32	34, 58					
3.0	11	58						
4.0	22	32						
5.0	11							
6.0	21							
7.1	11	45						
7.2	11	58						
7.3	11							
7.4	11	58						
7.5	11	58						
7.6	11							
7.7	23	51, 35						
7.8	11							
7.9	11	58						
8.0	58, 11							
8.1	71							
8.2	11	58						
9.0	11	35	58					
10.0	11	58						
11.0	11	42	32	34				
12.0	11	58, 32	62, 42					
13.0	11	58, 51	32	58				
14.0	12							
15.0	12	34						
16.0	33, 22	34, 58						
17.0	11							
17.1	11							
17.2	11	58						
18.0	11	31	34, 58					

SAMPLE CODED INTERVIEW

III. Questionnaire Used in Sample Interview

Spring 1973

Interviewer
(Name or Label)   *Susan Williams*
                          Jackson, Michigan   Condition: ⊠

                                                                 Q

Your
Interview
Number   *37*   Time
                                    Interview _____ A.M.
                                    Starts: *7:00*   P.M.

INTRODUCTION

I am from the Survey Research Center, and we're doing a survey for the

_____.

The purpose of this survey is to obtain information about sicknesses and other
health problems the people have now or have had in the past 12 months.

Q1. Our first question is about your present health in general. Within the
     last month, that is since _*May 15*_ , have you had any sicknesses, ill-
     nesses, injuries, or any other problems with your health?

     Nothing — I had a little flu, 3 weeks ago (RQ) I hurt
     my arm, lifting a heavy box, strained my elbow & shoulder
     some.

     Q1a. Please tell me something (more) about health problems you have had
           during the last month.

           I had a headache, that's all.

SAMPLE CODED INTERVIEW

Q2. Now we would like to ask you how you feel these days. In general, how is your health now? Would you say your health is excellent, very good, good, fair, or poor?

| ~~EXCELLENT~~ | VERY GOOD | GOOD | FAIR | POOR |

Q3. What kinds of problems do you have with your health? What's wrong with your health?

I have a little arthritis, once in a while, doctor said I have slight tendency to high blood pressure. besides that, I'm in fine shape.

Now we would like to know how your health compares with others.

Q4. What about <u>physical fitness</u>. Compared to (men/women) your own age, would you say you are much more <u>physically fit</u>, more, about the same, less physically fit, or much less fit?

| MUCH MORE | ~~MORE~~ | SAME | LESS | MUCH LESS |

Q5. Now about <u>energy</u>. Compared to (men/women) your own age, would you say you have much more <u>energy</u>, more energy, about the same, less, or much less energy?

| MUCH MORE | MORE | ~~SAME~~ | LESS | MUCH LESS |

Q6. What about <u>enjoying life</u>. Compared to (men/women) your own age, would you say you are enjoying life much more, more, about the same, less, or much less?

| MUCH MORE | MORE | ~~SAME~~ | LESS | MUCH LESS |

SAMPLE CODED INTERVIEW

Q7. Here are some other health conditions you may have had any time <u>during</u> <u>the past year</u> even though they may not bother you now. Have you had any of the following conditions at any time during the last 12 months, that is, since (MONTH) of 1972?

```
┌─────────────────────────────────────────────────────────────────────┐
│                                                                       │
│   PAY ATTENTION TO YOUR VOICE INFLECTION WHILE READING THE LIST       │
│                                                                       │
└─────────────────────────────────────────────────────────────────────┘
```

		YES	NO	DON'T KNOW
7.1.	Skin trouble?		X	
7.2.	Rheumatism or arthritis?	X		
7.3.	Bronchitis?		X	
7.4.	Sinus trouble?			*has colds, ok if sinus trouble*
7.5.	Trouble getting to sleep?		X	
7.6.	Trouble with teeth?		X	
7.7.	Cold or flu?	X		
7.8.	Heart trouble?		X	
7.9.	Allergy?		X	

Q8. Is there anything about the kind of work you do or the conditions you work in that you regard as dangerous or as bad for your health?

┌──────────┐   ┌──────────┐
│ 1. Y̶E̶S̶ │   │ 5. NO   │ ── GO TO Q9
└──────────┘   └──────────┘

Q8a. What is this (are these)? *only one kind of thing (I'm a maint. eng.) have to clean with chemicals every once in a while, little worried about the fumes the chemicals give off - that's about all.*

Q8b. Would you say this is (these are) a serious or slight problem for you?

┌────────────────────────┐   ┌────────────────────────┐
│ 1. SERIOUS PROBLEM   │   │ 2. SLI̶G̶H̶T̶ PROBLEM   │
└────────────────────────┘   └────────────────────────┘

SAMPLE CODED INTERVIEW

ASK EVERYONE

Q9. Think about the kind of activities which you usually do in your (work/
housework/school work). Do you have enough strength and energy to do
these things as well as you would like?

1. ~~YES~~		5. NO		OTHER_____

Q10. What about (five) years in the future? Do you think you will have
enough strength and energy to do your (work/housework) as well as now?

1. ~~YES~~		5. NO		OTHER_____

Q11. What about activities which you enjoy in your free time, such as the
things you like to do either alone, with your family, or with friends?
First, what are some of the free time activities which you most enjoy
doing?

_in summer, like to play golf, in winter I bowl
2 things I think I enjoy most._

Q12. Thinking about these activities which you enjoy, do you have enough
strength and energy to do them as much and as well as you would like?

1. ~~YES~~		5. NO		OTHER_____

Q13. Do you have enough strength and energy to do these free time activities
as much and as well as you did them (five/ten) years ago?

1. YES	7	5. NO		OTHER _Not quite as well_

SAMPLE CODED INTERVIEW

Q14. Have you visited a doctor in the past month, that is since _May 15_ ?

[~~YES~~]   [NO]

about shoulder

Q15. Have you been in a hospital in the last 12 months, that is, since

June 15, 1971 ?

[YES]   [~~NO~~] *not since 5 years ago*

Q16. Are you married, separated, divorced, widowed, or have you never been married?

[1. ~~MARRIED~~]   [2. SEPARATED]   [3. DIVORCED]   [4. WIDOWED]

[5. NEVER MARRIED]

Q17. What is the highest grade of school or year of college you completed?

[00] [01] [02] [03] [04] [05] [06] [07] [08] [09] [10] [11] [~~12~~]

> Q17a. Did you get a high school graduation diploma or pass a high school equivalence test?
>
> [1. ~~YES~~]   [5. NO]

College: [13] [14] [15] [16] [17]

Q17b. Do you have a college degree?   [1. YES]   [5. ~~NO~~]

INAP
What degree is that? _____

83

SAMPLE CODED INTERVIEW

Q18.   (CARD 3)   To get an accurate picture of people's financial situation,
       we need to know the income of all the families we interview.   Would
       you please tell me the letter on this card that indicates how much
       income you and your family received from all sources during last year,
       1972; I mean before taxes or any deductions?

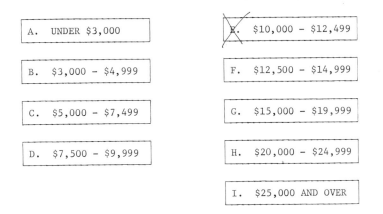

A.   UNDER $3,000

B. $3,000 - $4,999

C. $5,000 - $7,499

D. $7,500 - $9,999

E. $10,000 - $12,499

F. $12,500 - $14,999

G. $15,000 - $19,999

H. $20,000 - $24,999

I. $25,000 AND OVER

CHAPTER 9

SAMPLE ANALYSIS OF INTERVIEWER PERFORMANCE

The data shown here represent two analyses. The first is based on 60 interviews which were conducted by the Survey Research Center national interviewing staff. These interviews do not constitute in any sense, a sample; they were merely conducted in areas in which supervisors had a tape recorder readily available at the time of the study. All of the interviews were based on the same questionnaire, and the number of interviews per interviewer ranged from one to five. This analysis follows the pattern described earlier in Chapter 5 on the feedback of information to interviewers.

The questionnaire contained both open and closed questions. Table 9-1 shows the general classes of activity, and the pattern of interviewers' behaviors. The ranges of amounts for each activity are wide. The variability among interviewers which this indicates is probably attributable both to the general tendencies of each interviewer and to adaptations which they make in their behavior to suit a particular respondent.

Table 9-2 shows the percentage of each major class of behaviors which was coded as acceptable and unacceptable. In this group of interviews, approximately three-quarters of the activity was acceptable, and a sizable 25 % was judged to be unacceptable. The ranges are startling, especially in light of the fact that one interviewer asked only slightly over 10% of the questions correctly. In addition, at least one person used over one-third unacceptable probes. It can also be seen from this Table that the proportion of unacceptable behavior is larger for the "other" behaviors which are less frequent and more difficult in training than for the basic question-asking and probing.

In considering these averages, one should not automatically blame interviewers for poor performances. While poor interviewers certainly constitute a major source of problems, and while these figures may well indicate a need either for additional training, or even for the discharge of some interviewers who are at the extreme end of the range of poor behavior, there is another major source of difficulty: the questionnaire itself. Our analysis shows that the wording of some questions is so complicated or awkward, that a high proportion of the errors in question-asking occurs in conjunction with relatively few questions. In these cases, the fault does not lie entirely with the interviewers; they have been given a very difficult task. Often the wording of the question does not convey the stated objective of the question and no amount of repetition or non-directive probing will enable the interviewer to obtain the needed information. The interviewer must then either accept a response he knows is inadequate or use a directive probe to compensate for the inadequacy of the question.* The extreme ranges shown for some of the activities suggest that, in some cases, the interviewer may have had either a particularly easy or a particularly difficult respondent, and the patterns may be a reflection of that quality rather than of the interviewer's usual behavior.

In the second stage of analysis, we coded from eight to twelve interviews for each of four interviewers who were working on a regular national sample survey in order to obtain information on the stability of activities. These four interviewers were selected simply because a tape recorder was available to them. Tables 9-3 and 9-4 show data which are comparable to those in Tables 9-1 and 9-2 for these four interviewers individually. There is considerably more stability in the averages for these interviewers, but the range for each is still rather large. This implies that one should be cautious in judging the quality of all interviewers' work on the basis of the work of one or two interviewers. A comparison of the average activities for the percent acceptable or unacceptable also shows differences between the two groups. This may reflect either differences in the type or degree of difficulty of the questionnaires which were used or differences in the interviewers' training and expertise or it may merely reflect the fact that this is a small sample which was not selected randomly.

The variability in range in activity should not be ignored, however, in evaluating interviewer performance because it may mean that an interviewer has a problem in interviewing a particular type of respondent (from a particular age, income, education, or racial group). When there are extremes, one should examine the interview situation during the poor performance and determine what might be done in order to avoid similar situations in the future.

---

*These findings suggest the possibility of using a behavior coding system as a basis for evaluating the questions during the pretest. The writers are at present developing such a system.

SAMPLE ANALYSIS OF INTERVIEWER PERFORMANCE

Table 9-1

Means and Ranges of Interviewer Activity
(30 interviewers)

Activity	Average % for all Interviewers	Percentage Range for all Interviewers
Question asking	69.6%	47.1 - 90.2%
Probing	23.4	7.4 - 35.4
Other	8.0	0 - 14.4
	100.0%	

Table 9-2

Means and Ranges of Interviewers Acceptable and Unacceptable
Activity
(30 interviewers)

Activity	Average % for all Interviewers	Percentage Range for all Interviewers
Question asking		
Acceptable	78.6%	13.2 - 96.4%
Unacceptable	21.4	2.5 - 86.8
	100.0%	
Probing		
Acceptable	79.8	61.7 - 98.0%
Unacceptable	20.2	2.0 - 38.3
	100.0%	
Other		
Acceptable	53.0%	28.5 - 100%
Unacceptable	47.0	0 - 76.0
	100.0%	

Table 9-3

Average Percent of All Activity for Four Experienced Interviewers

Activity	All Interviewers' Average	Individual Interviewer's Averages			
		1	2	3	4
Question asking (Range)	78.7% (49.8-97.4)	80.7% (70.1-95.1)	86.8% (68.5-97.4)	72.2% (62.8-96.8)	75.5% (49.8-93.9)
Probing (Range)	17.9 (1.3-45.6)	14.7 (3.3-24.5)	11.3 (2.1-27.8)	25.5 (1.2-32.6)	19.5 (5.6-35.6)
Other (Range)	2.1 (0-6.6)	3.2 (1.2-5.5)	.8 (0-2.8)	1.2 (0-3.8)	3.3 (0-6.6)
Other (skips) (Range)	1.3 (0-7.2)	1.4 (0-7.2)	1.1 (0-5.9)	1.1 (0-5.9)	1.7 (0-4.9)
Total Activity	100%	100%	100%	100%	100%
No. of Interviews	35	10	9	8	8

Table 9-4

Percentage Distribution of Acceptable and Unacceptable Activity for Four Interviewers Based on 8-12 Interviews Each

Activity	All Interviewers' Average	Individual Interviewer's Averages			
		1	2	3	4
Question asking					
Acceptable	95%	85%	98%	96%	94%
(Range)	(75-100)	(75-99)	(96-100)	(78-99)	(78-100)
Unacceptable	5%	11%	2%	4%	6%
(Range)	(0-24)	(5-24)	(0-4)	(0-22)	(0-21)
Total	100%	100%	100%	100%	100%
Probing					
Acceptable	89%	91%	90%	92%	88%
(Range)	(67-100)	(80-100)	(75-100)	(80-100)	(67-100)
Unacceptable	11%	9%	10%	8%	12%
(Range)	(0-34)	(0-19)	(0-25)	(0-20)	(0-34)
Total	100%	100%	100%	100%	100%
Other					
Acceptable	48%	41%	50%	57%	53%
(Range)	(0-100)	(0-80)	(0-100)	(0-100)	(0-100)
Unacceptable	52%	59%	50%	43%	47%
(Range)	(0-100)	(20-100)	(0-100)	(0-100)	(0-100)
Total	100%	100%	100%	100%	100%

CHAPTER 10

INSTRUCTIONS TO INTERVIEWERS*

PURPOSE

You have been asked to use a tape recorder in order to obtain a complete record of your interviews. The tapes of these recordings will be used in a new procedure which has been developed for coding the number and kinds of behaviors which occur during an interview. The information obtained from this coding provides a basis for training new interviewers and improving the performance of those already trained.

The following instructions have been compiled to facilitate your use of the recorder.

INTRODUCING THE RECORDER:

Simply explain to the respondent that the recorder is used in order to obtain a complete record of the interview, and that you would like to use it if that is acceptable to him. Most respondents do not have any preconceived notions about interview situations so that if the interviewer uses a tape recorder as if it were an integral part of the interview, the respondent will usually agree to its presence.

EQUIPMENT AND PLACEMENT:

Check to ensure that the machine is working properly BEFORE you leave for the interview. If you are using a cadmium battery pack (a rechargeable pack), be sure it is fully charged. If you are using flashlight batteries, be sure that they are fresh, and always carry the electric power cord for your machine "just in case. . . ."

Some interviewers prefer to carry their tape recorders in a shopping bag in order to avoid possible theft. You may carry the machine in any manner you please as long as it is protected from moisture and extreme cold.

---

*The material presented here is a sample of the type of instructions given to interviewers when they first begin using tape recorders.

LOCATION OF THE MICROPHONE:

The location of the microphone is very important. If you have a new SONY with a round microphone, set it on the plastic stand (included with it) and point the microphone to the side between you and the respondent. If you point the microphone directly at the respondent, it will not pick up your voice very well. If you have the older SONY, you will have a *square* or rectangular microphone. Set this microphone flat with the face pointing at the ceiling. If your respondent has a very soft voice you may have to move the microphone closer to him. Remember to speak loud enough so that your voice will record well too.

Do *not* put the microphone either on or right next to the recorder or it will pick up the sound of the motor. Put the microphone on a soft surface such as your scarf or a pile of paper, or bring a household sponge for this purpose, if possible.

Try to place the microphone as far as possible from other noises in the room such as TV, children, etc., but as close as possible to you and the respondent. Practice recording at home while your radio or TV is on since some homes you interview in will have these disturbances.

Use 90-minute cassette tapes. The shorter ones are not adequate for a whole interview, and longer ones tend to become tangled. These tapes are usually supplied to an interviewer upon request. If you have to buy them, they should be entered on your expense voucher so that you can be reimbursed. We prefer TDK, Maxell and BASF brand cassettes. Bargain tapes usually produce bargain quality recordings.

Since each side of the cassette records for 45 minutes, it is a good idea to write yourself a note in the questionnaire at a convenient place to turn the tape. Do not bother rewinding the tape to the beginning of side 2, but remember when you listen to the tape that there will be some blank tape at the beginning of side 2. After you turn the tape, do not turn the machine on and off during the interview unless there are lengthy interruptions.

OPERATING YOUR TAPE RECORDER:

Practice using your recorder at home and during your practice interview. Afterwards, you may record a regular interview on the tape which you used for practice.

USING THE MICROPHONE:

Your recorder will have several plug holes on the front and the microphone must be plugged into the correct ones. The holes are labeled "mic," "aux" and "ear"; plug the mike into the two holes labeled "mic." If you are not certain which are the correct holes, practice recording and listening to what you have recorded until you are.

92

TO RECORD:

On your recorder there is a button marked "Record" and a button marked "Play." Both buttons must be pushed at the same time for the machine to record. Be sure the microphone is plugged in.

REMOTE CONTROL WITH THE MICROPHONE:

The microphone has a small "ON/OFF" button. After you have set up the recorder, this button must be set to "ON." If you push it to "OFF," the machine will not record. If you wish, you can set up the recorder to record before you leave your home and use the button on the microphone to operate the recorder while you are in the respondent's home.

REVIEW:

Because of the time it takes, you should not check your questionnaires against the information on the tape recordings. You are encouraged, however, to listen to some of your tapes to review your performance. While you are listening, "observe" your own interviewing technique: Did you read all of the questions exactly as they were worded? Did you probe when necessary? Were the objectives for each question met? Did you read slowly and clearly, giving your respondent time for a considered reply? Did you approach the respondent in a professional manner, showing neither approval nor disapproval, rewarding him positively for his performance as a respondent rather than for the responses which he gave? The tape recording enables you to evaluate your own performance in a way which is impossible to manage when you are in the midst of an interview. The tape, in effect, gives you a chance to observe yourself.

ADDITIONAL NOTES AND TAPE RECORDING INFORMATION:

Microphones

There are two different types of microphones for the SONY, one *round* and the other *square*. (Also see LOCATION OF THE MICROPHONE.)

Batteries

The SONY tape recorder has a rechargeable battery pack *and* a cord for plugging the recorder into a regular wall outlet. The batteries will last all day, but they must be *recharged each night*. To recharge them, you must plug the recorder into a wall outlet in your home for 12 hours. Then the recorder will be good for the next day. Although it takes 12 hours to recharge completely used batteries, a full 12 hours of recharging will usually not be necessary. If you are interviewing in the evening and then again the next morning so that you have less than 12 hours for recharging, you can check the battery condition dial to see whether the batteries are charged enough. (If you should forget to recharge your batteries, you can use a pack of flashlight batteries in your recorder. These are good for only one day (4 interviews) and then must be replaced.)

The recorders also have a cord to plug into the wall outlet. If your batteries run down unexpectedly while you are at an interview, you can use the cord to plug your recorder into an outlet in the respondent's home. This is not recommended, however, since the location of the outlet is often inconvenient.

Remote Control

Remember that your machine will not work when the microphone is plugged in *unless* the mike switch is in the "ON" position. Always check this switch before you assume either that the batteries are dead or that something else is wrong with the machine.

Volume Control

Most SONY recorders self-adjust for volume during recording. The volume control only adjusts the volume for play-back. These machines will usually pick up any noise, no matter how faint, so that it is important to place the microphone as close as possible to the respondent and yourself, and as far as possible from background noise.

Cold Weather

The tape recorder should be protected from extreme temperatures. Cold will not harm the tape recorder permanently, but a cold machine will work slowly and produce poor quality tapes. If your machine has been out in the cold for some time, it should be allowed a 15-30 minute warm-up time before you use it.

Practice Interview & Mailing Tapes

Send the practice tape and practice interview to your local coordinator or supervisor. Before you mail the tapes, write identifying information on the tape cassette itself, and also on the mailing box. Identifying information includes:

> Your name
> Your City and State
> Your Interview Number (as it appears on the cover sheet)
> (Also indicate which side is side 1 and which is side 2.)
> Do *not* include any respondent identification

INSTRUCTIONS TO INTERVIEWERS

When you get home, plug your tape recorder in and "rewind" your completed tapes. If you have a recording machine which cannot be plugged into regular house current electricity, do not bother to rewind the tapes.

If you used only one side of the tape, *rewind* it to the beginning. If you used both sides of the tape, run the second side *forward* as far as it will go.

Place the tape cassette in the box in which it came. Send it with the completed interview to your supervisor. In order to avoid tearing the mailing envelope, send only 3 tapes per regular mailing envelope.

IMPORTANT: Place the tape boxes BETWEEN the completed interviews (sandwich-style) in the mailing envelope.

POINTS TO REMEMBER

Be sure recorder is running and set to *record* when you begin.

Do not set microphone on the recorder.

Place the microphone as close to both of you as possible.

Set microphone where it will not be bumped during recording, preferably on a soft surface .

Put your name, city, state and interview number on each tape cassette when it is completed (and indicate which is side 1 and which is side 2). Also put identification information on the tape box.

Remember to recharge your recorder at night.

IMPORTANT: Poor quality tape recordings increase study costs. A recording which contains excessive background noise (e.g., the TV set) or fails to pick up the respondent's voice clearly causes great problems for the listener.

Please do everything you can to get good quality tape recordings.

CHAPTER 11

PROGRAM DOCUMENTATION*

*TIMBO DISTRIBUTION TAPE***

The TIMBO distribution tape contains load modules for the programs TIMBO and NKTIMBO in the form of an OS unloaded partitioned dataset. The tape is 9-track, 800 bpi density, and has IBM standard labels. The volume serial number is TIMBO, and the modules are in the first and only dataset. The dataset carries the name TIMLIB, the same name as the library to be created. The control cards indicated below make use of the IBM utility IEHMOVE to create a partitioned dataset TIMLIB and load the two programs into it. The device types DISK, TAPE and 310l may have to be changed at other installations, as well as the disk volume serial number ISRB, which is specific to the Institute for Social Research.

```
//   EXEC PGM=IEHMOVE
//SYSPRINT DD SYSOUT=A
//SYSUTI DD UNIT=SYSDA,SPACE=(TRK,(100,10))
//DISK DD UNIT=DISK,VOL=SER=ISRB,DISP=OLD
//TAPE DD UNIT=TAPE,VOL=SER=TIMBO,DISP=OLD
//SYSIN DD *
  COPY DSNAME=TIMLIB,FROM=TAPE=TIMBO,TO=310l=ISRB,
     FROMDD=TAPE
/*
```

I. TIMBO

TIMBO is a program which prepares standard OSIRIS files of frequencies and transition frequencies for behavior codes, plus associated descriptor data. It can perform filtering, bracketing, and aggregating in the process. TIMBO is written in FORTRAN, and has several OSIRIS subroutines in both FORTRAN and IBM Assembly language for use under OS and OS/VS. The program requires 110 K of core.

---

*Peter Solenberger was the sole author of all materials presented in this chapter.

**The distribution tape can be obtained from the authors for approximately $7.50 (processing fee) plus the cost of a 9-track tape (if not provided by the purchaser).

PROGRAM DOCUMENTATION

A. Input

1. Data prepared by the program NKTIMBO (see Section II of this Chapter) and sorted into the desired sequence on either tape or disk. (See the note on sorting input data at the end of this section.)

2. Control cards.

B. Output

1. *Dictionary and data files* (up to 4) on either tape or disk. Variables for the output files consist of descriptor variables selected by user from the input descriptor variables, plus frequencies and transition frequencies for behavior codes selected by user. Transition frequency is the frequency with which code A follows code B within the specified portion of the interview. Behavior codes may be either bracketed or excluded before frequencies are measured.

2. *Printout*

   a. All control cards are printed. If an error is detected, processing terminates and an error message is printed. One of the following numbers is printed to indicate that the corresponding error has been discovered.

      1 Wrong keyword or format in global or local parameter card.

      2 Error either in reading first record of input data file or in writing output dictionary.

      3 No identification variables or identification variable number out of range (identification variable numbers can range from 1 to the number of descriptor variables in the input data file).

      4 Information variable number out of range (information variable numbers also can range from 1 to the number of descriptor variables in the input data file).

      5 Filter variable number out of range (filter variable numbers range from 1 to the number of descriptor variables in the input data file, the same as identification and information variables).

      6 Error in local parameters; either no output file name given or "continuous-type" aggregation level break higher than "summation-type" aggregation level break.

      7 Error in behavior code list (card column of error also printed).

      9 Error in naming descriptor variables for output file.

      10 Error in naming behavior codes for output file.

98

b. During processing, two kinds of errors might occur: sequence errors and I/0 errors. In either case, the program terminates with an error message indicating the case number in which the error occurred.

c. If the program goes to successful completion, the number of records which were input and output for each file is printed.

C. Setup

1. For users of OSIRIS:

```
//    EXEC OSIRIS, LIB =(catalogued library containing TIMBO),
                LIB1=(catalogued library containing OSIRIS)
//DATAx  DD   parameters for input data file
              (See note on data flow from NKTIMBO to TIMBO at
              the end of this section)
//DICTy  DD   parameters for output dictionary file } up to 4
//DATAy  DD   parameters for output data file        } output files
//SETUP  DD   *
$RUN  TIMBO
```

1. Global filter card (optional).
2. Global label card.
3. Global parameter card.
4. Local filter card (optional). }
5. Local label card.   } up to 4 sets for
6. Local parameter card.   } 4 output files.
7. Local behavior code list.   }
/* 8. Names for variables (optional).

2. For users not using OSIRIS:

```
//    EXEC PGM=TIMBO
//STEPLIB   DD   parameters for library containing TIMBO
//DATAx     DD   parameters for sorted input data file
//DICTy     DD   parameters for output dictionary file } up to 4
//DATAy     DD   parameters for output data file        } output
//FTO1FOO1 DD   *
```

1. Global filter card (optional).
2. Global label card.
3. Global parameter card.

4. Local filter card (optional). ⎫
5. Local label card. ⎬ up to 4 sets for
6. Local parameter card. ⎪ 4 output files.
7. Local behavior code list. ⎭
8. Names for variables (optional).

/*

D. Control Cards

1. Global filter card (optional): See OSIRIS Appendix C*
2. Global label card: 1-80 columns, punched free-form
3. Global parameter card: Keywords (defaults underlined)
   are separated by commas or blanks; list is terminated by
   an asterisk.

   INFILE=IN/xxxx   Allow user to specify a 1 to 4 character
                               input ddname suffix

   ID=(variable list)   Specifies descriptor variables used to identify
                           records; data must be sorted in same order as
   ID variable list; ID variables are numbered
   according to their positions in descriptor segment of input data record (see note on sorting
   input data).

   IF=(variable list)   Optional parameter; allows inclusion of descriptor variables not to be checked for sequence
   but only to be used as information; IF variables are also numbered according to their positions in descriptor segment of input data
   record.

4. Local filter card (optional): See OSIRIS Appendix C*
5. Local label card: 1-80 columns, punched free-form
6. Local parameter card: Keywords (defaults underlined)
   are separated by commas or blanks; list is terminated by asterisk.

   OUTFILE=xxxx   Specifies 1 to 4 character output file ddname
   suffix for this analysis packet (no default;
   ddname suffix *must* be supplied).

   PRINT=DICT/NODICT   Allows user to specify whether output
   dictionary for this file is to be printed.

---

*There is a section describing the use of filters in the Appendix of the OSIRIS III
User's Manual, Volume 1.

AGGREG=(m,n) Specifies descriptor variables which are to signal level breaks for "continuous-type" and "summation-type" aggregating. All records occurring between changes in the value of variable m are to be treated as a *continuous* sequence of behaviors. Frequencies for all continuous sequences of behaviors from records occurring between changes in the value of n are to be summed to give aggregated frequencies. Variable n must occur later than variable m in identifier variable list and must be more minor in the sort sequence (no defaults; both m and n *must* be supplied).

OPT=<u>TWO</u>/ONE Specifies frequency table option; ONE indicates *only* frequencies for specified behavior codes; TWO indicates *both* individual code frequencies and transition code frequencies.

7. *Local behavior code list:* User must supply a list of valid behavior codes. Codes may be combined and renumbered while being listed. Codes not included in list will be skipped over when they occur in input records. Codes may be listed either individually or in ranges. Codes surrounded by brackets are to be renumbered according to rule: <old codes> = new code. List must be in ascending order of *output* code, and must be terminated by an asterisk.

Example: <1-5,9, 20-29,31>=99*

Eight output codes will be produced: 1,2,3,4,5,8,9,99. All input codes will be disregarded, except the following: 1,2,3,4,5,8,9,20, 21,22,23,24,25,26,27,28,29,31.

Note: One output file will be produced for each set of the local control cards. After the first packet, subsequent packets may omit the PRINT, AGGR, and OPT parameters (but *not* the OUTF parameter). This will cause the program to use the options selected for the previous packet. Also, after the first packet, subsequent packets may omit the behavior code list, supplying an asterisk in its place. This will cause the program to use the behavior codes selected for the preceding packet. Up to four packets may be included.

8. *Names for variables.* If default names are unsatisfactory, user may provide names for descriptor variables and behavior-code frequency variables, but not for transition frequencies. Descriptor variables must be named first, then behavior code frequencies. The following three types of cards are needed:

101

a.   NAME   Word 'name' in Col. 1-4 signifies that user-supplied variable names are to follow.

b.   DC=var,N='name'*   Gives descriptor variable number (must be in the range 1-100 and, if it is to be used, must be included in either the ID or IF list) and name to be used.

c.   BV=code,N='name'*   Gives output behavior code number (must be in the range 0-999 and, if it is to be used, must be a valid output code for at least one of the packets) and name to be used.

Ascending order must be maintained both within descriptor variables and within behavior-code frequency variables, although either group of names may be omitted. Variable names are provided *once* for each run. They apply to all files in which the variable occurs.

Behavior-code frequency variables will be given new variable numbers in the range 1000-1999 to preserve ascending variable numbers for dictionary. Each output behavior code will have 1000 added to it. First behavior at question level and last behavior will be given code of 1000 and variable number of 2000. Transition frequencies will be given variable numbers beginning with number 2001. Transition frequencies will be put out *by rows* (i.e., all "to" codes will be listed before "from" code changes).

The default variable names are as follows:

(1)   Descriptor variables:

      'DESCRIPTOR VAR. nnnn'

where nnnn is the original descriptor variable number in the range 1-1000.

(2)   Behavior-code frequency variables:

      'FREQ: BEHAVIOR CODE nnnn'

where nnnn is the output code in the range 0-1000.

(3)   Transition frequency variables:

      'FREQ: CODE mmmm to nnnn'

where mmmm is the 'from' code and 'nnnn' is the 'to' code, both in the range 0-1000.

Note on sorting input data: Before TIMBO is run, the input data must be sorted in ascending order of the identifying variables. The first identifying variable begins in column 9 of the input data record. Each variable has a field-width of 4. For instance, the following SORT control card would be needed for an identifying variable list, ID=(V4,V3,V2,V1):

SORT FIELDS=(21,4,A,17,4,A,13,4,A,9,4,A),FORMAT=FI

Note that the first eight bytes of the record are taken up by system and program record descriptor words, and that the records have a fixed-length format, length 4.

The following JCL is needed to chain the sort with NKTIMBO and TIMBO under OSIRIS:

```
//SORTIN    DD   VOL=REF=*.FTO4FOO1,DSN=*.FTO4FOO1,
//               DCB=(RECFM=VSB,BLKSIZE=2004,LRECL=
                 4404)
//SORTOUT  DD   VOL=REF=*.FTO4FOO1,DSN=*.FTO4FOO1,
//               DCB=(RECFM=VSB,BLKSIZE=2004,LRECL=
                 4404)
//DATAIN   DD   VOL=REF=*.FTO4FOO1,DSN=*.FTO4FOO1
```

The backward references in SORTOUT and DATAIN can be changed to create a permanent file.

II. NKTIMBO

NKTIMBO is the variable-length-record "card-to-tape" and edit program. It reads, edits, converts to binary, and writes variable length records, such as those from interview behavior data. The program is written in IBM assembly language for use under OS and OS/VS. The program requires 40 K of core.

A. Input

1. *Behavior and descriptor data* on cards, tape, or disk.

    a. *Ganged descriptor records.* Records are marked by a '?' in column 1 and may be continued from one physical record to the next by omission of a '?' in column 1 of succeeding records (or an '*' indicating behavior data records. See below.). They contain descriptor information to be ganged into subsequent behavior data records until next ganged descriptor record is reached.

    b. *Behavior data record.* Records are marked by an '*' in column 1 and may be continued from one physical record to the next by omission of a '?' or an '*' in column 1 of succeeding records. They contain descriptor and behavior information for each output record.

2. *Control Cards*

B. Output

1. *Valid behavior data* on tape or disk containing the following information in four-byte, fixed-point binary words:

   a. The (fixed) number of descriptor variables in the record. One word.

   b. The descriptor variables, including ganged variables, in the record. From one to 100 words.

   c. The (variable) number of behavior codes in the record. One word.

   d. The behavior codes in the record. From one to 1000 words.

2. *Error records* on card, tape, or disk. All physical records affected by an error in any one physical record are output to this file and are not output to the valid behavior data file. An error in a ganged descriptor record affects all subsequent behavior data records until next ganged descriptor record is reached. An error in any one physical record affects all other physical records logically associated with it.

3. *Printout*

   a. All control cards are printed. When an error is detected, one of the following numbers is printed on the line following the card in error to indicate that the corresponding error has occurred.

Number	Error
0	Excessive *physical* record length on input data file (max. 256 bytes per *physical* record).
1	Control statement too long (control statements may span cards but may not have more than 800 bytes, *excluding* blanks).
2.	Continuation portion of excessively long control statement.
3	Premature end-of-file; no behavior fields described.
4	Unrecognizable control card.
5	Excessive number of descriptor variables (max. 100, including ganged descriptor variables).
7	Control card number field too long; max field lengths:

variable field origin -5
variable field length -5
variable valid constant length$-$field length
               plus 1

| 8 | Zero field length. |

9	Wrong delimiter for variable field origin.
10	Non-positive variable field origin.
11	Wrong delimiter for variable field length.
12	Non-positive variable field length.
13	Excessive variable field length (max. 10 digits) in data record.
14	Variable field extending beyond maximum permissible length of data record (1600 bytes).
15	Behavior code fields overlap with descriptor variable fields.
16	Wrong delimiter for constants.
17	High end of range not greater than low end of range.
18	High end of range or single value not greater than previous high end of range or single value.
19	Length of constant table exceeded.

b. Error data records are printed with a number to left of physical record image indicating sequence number (from beginning of file) of physical record, and a number to right of physical record image indicating column of *logical* record in which error occurred.

c. A summary is printed of number of physical input records, number of valid logical output records, and number of physical error output records.

C. Setup

For users of OSIRIS:

```
JOB card
//      EXEC OSIRIS, LIB=(catalogued library containing NKTIMBO),
                 LIB1=(catalogued library containing OSIRIS)
//FTO3FOO1 DD  *,DCB=(RECFM=FB,LRECL=80,BLKSIZE=80,
                 BUFNO=2)
     .
     .
     .
     input data cards
     .
     .
     .
/*
//FTO8FOO1 DD   parameters for error output file; either
               SYSOUT=B, DUMMY, or a disk or tape file for
               later use (include DCB)
```

```
//FTO4FOO1 DD    parameters for valid record output file on tape
                 or disk (exclude DCB)

//SETUP     DD   *
$RUN NKTIMBO
    .
    .
    .
    input control cards
    .
    .
    .
/*
```

For users not using OSIRIS:

```
//    EXEC   PGM = NKTIMBO
//STEPLIB   DD    parameters for library containing NKTIMBO
//FTO1FOO1 DD     *
    .
    .
    .
    input control cards
    .
    .
    .
/*
//FTO3FOO1 DD     parameters for input file (may be '*' if input
                  data cards follow)
//FTO4FOO1 DD     parameters for valid record output file on
                  tape or disk (exclude DCB)
//FTO6FOO1 DD     SYSOUT=A
//FTO8FOO1 DD     parameters for error output file,
                      either SYSOUT=B, DUMMY or a disk or
                      tape file for later use (include DCB)
```

D. Control Cards

Control cards are of three types:

1. DC=(origin, length, [constant list]). This control card specifies the field origin and field length for a descriptor variable. The descriptor variables may be either right- or left-justified in the field, but they may not be all-blank. An optional constant list of ranges and single values can be included for wild code checking.

    Example: DC=(10,4,1000-1020,1030,1050-1060,1090)

2. DC=SET. This control card indicates (a) that the set of descriptor control cards processed *before* it is to be considered a complete description of *ganged* records for the run such as demographic information, and (b) that the descriptor control cards processed *after* it refer to the descriptor variables which are attached to each behavior record, such as question number.

106

3. BV=(origin, length, [constant list]). This control card specifies the field origin of the *first* behavior code and the field length for *all* behavior codes. A behavior code may be either right-or left-justified in the field. A blank field indicates end-of-behavior for the question. Subsequent behavior codes are assumed to follow immediately after the first one. An optional constant list of ranges and single values can be included for wild-code checking.

    Example: BV=(15,2,0-20,99)

III. SOURCE PROGRAM TIMBO

EXTERNAL SYMBOL DICTIONARY

PAGE 1
15.30 7/27/74

SYMBOL	TYPE	ID	ADDR	LENGTH	LD ID
TIMBO	SD	01	000000	CC48B8	

```
LOC       OBJECT CODE        ADDR1   ADDR2    STMT    SOURCE STATEMENT

                                               1            PRINT NOGEN
                                               2   TIMBO    START  0
000000    47FF 000C                  00C0C     3            B     12(15)
000004    07                                   4            DC    X'07'
000005    D5D2E3C9D4C2D6                        5            DC    C'NKTIMBO'
00000C    90EC D00C                  0000C     6            STM   14,12,12(13)
000010    18BF                                 7            LR    11,15
000000                                         8            USING TIMBO,11
000012    184D                                 9            LR    4,13
000014    41D0 B9B8                  00988    10            LA    13,SAVE
000018    50D4 0004                  00004    11            ST    4,4(13)
00001C    50D4 0008                  00008    12            ST    13,8(4)
                                              13   *
000020    9204 BC08                  00C08    14            MVI   TAB,X'04'
000024    D2FE BC09 BC08    00C09    00C08    15            MVC   TAB+1(255),TAB
00002A    9203 BC65                  00C65    16            MVI   TAB+93,X'33'
00002E    9202 BC68                  00C68    17            MVI   TAB+96,X'32'
000032    9201 BC73                  00C73    18            MVI   TAB+107,X'01'
000036    D709 BCF8 BCF8    00CF8    00CF8    19            XC    TAB+240(10),TAB+240
                                              20   *
                                              21            OPEN  (CARDIN,(INPUT),PRINT,(OUTPUT),INTAPE,(INPUT))
00004E    D24D BA89 B80E    00A89    0080E    31            MVC   PRTAREA(78),HEAD
000054    D22A BAD7 BAD6    00AC7    0AD6     32            MVC   PRTAREA+78(43),PRTAREA+77
                                              33            PUT   PRINT,PRTAREA
000068    D206 BA89 BBDE    00A89    00BDE    35            MVC   PRTAREA(7),=C'- CARD '
00006E    D27D BA90 BA8F    00A90    00A8F    39            MVC   PRTAREA+7(126),PRTAREA+6
000074    4140 BA91                  00A91    40            LA    4,INAREA
000078    4120 000A                  0000A    41            LA    2,10
00007C    4130 BAE0                  00AE0    42            LA    3,INAREA+79
000080    D209 4000 BB88    00000    00B88    43            MVC   0(10,4),=C'1234567890'
000086    8742 B080                  00080    44            BXLE  4,2,*-6
                                              45            PUT   PRINT,PRTAREA
000098    92F0 BA89         00A89             50            MVI   PRTAREA,X'F0'
00009C    4110 0100                  00100    51            LA    1,-256
0000A0    4860 B8E6                  00BE6    52            LH    6,INTAPE+82
0000A4    1916                                53            CR    1,6
0000A6    4780 B0BE                  000BE    54            BNL   COLENCK
0000AA    1B11                                55            SR    1,1
0000AC    4210 B16D                  0016D    56            STC   1,CDERR-1
                                              57            CLOSE INTAPE
0000BA    47F0 B15C                  0015C    63            B     CDEOF
0000BE    1B00                                64   COLENCK  SR    0,0
0000C0    5810 BA0C         COADC             65            L     1,COLIM
0000C4    1D06                                66            DR    0,6
0000C6    5010 BA10                  00A10    67            S     1,CDMAXNO
0000CA    4111 0001                  00001    68            LA    1,1(1)
0000CE    5010 BA14                  00A14    69            ST    1,CDMAXNCP
0000D2    5860 BA64                  00A64    70            L     6,CNVEC
                                              71   *
0000D6    FA30 BA80 BBE5    00A80    00BE5    72   CDSTART  AP    COUNT,=P'1'
0000DC    F333 BA8B BAB0    00A8B    00AB0    73            UNPK  PRTAREA+2(4),COUNT
0000E2    96F0 BA8E                  00A8E    74            OI    PRTAREA+5,X'F0'
0000E6    4120 0001                  00001    75            LA    2,1
0000EA    4130 BAE0                  00AE0    76            LA    3,INAREA+79
0000EE    5870 BA74                  00A74    77            L     7,STMNT
```

109

PROGRAM DOCUMENTATION

LOC	OBJECT CODE	ADDR1	ADDR2	STMT	SOURCE	STATEMENT		
0000F2	4180 0001		00001	78		LA	8,1
0000F6	4197 063F		0063F	79		LA	9,1599(7)
				80	COREAD	GET	CARDIN,INAREA
				85		PUT	PRINT,PRTAREA
000116	9240 BA89	00A89		90		MVI	PRTAREA,X'40'
				91	*		
00011A	4110 BA91	00A91		92		LA	1,INAREA
00011E	9540 1000			93	COLOOP	CLI	0(1),X'40'
000122	4780 B14C		0014C	94		BE	CDCROSS
000126	D200 7000 1000		00000	95		MVC	0(1,7),0(1)
00012C	955D 1000			96		CLI	0(1),C')'
000130	4780 B1FE		001FE	97		BE	CDPROC
000134	95E3 1000			98		CLI	0(1),C'T'
000138	4780 B1FE		001FE	99		BE	CDPROC
00013C	8778 BA85	00A85	0014C	100		BXLE	7,8,CDCROSS
000140	92FF 8A85	00A85		101		MVI	LENSW,X'FF'
000144	41F0 0001		00001	102		LA	15,1
000148	47F0 B16E		0016E	103		B	CDERR
00014C	8712 B11E		0011E	104	CDCROSS	BXLE	1,2,COLOOP
000150	D204 BA8A BA89	00A8A	00A89	105		MVC	PRTAREA+1(5),PRTAREA
000156	47F0 B0FA		000FA	106		B	CDREAD
				107	*		
000166	940F B1A3	001A3		108	CDEOF	CLOSE	CARDIN
00016A	41F0 0003		00003	114		NI	BRERR+1,X'0F'
				115		LA	15,3
00016E	D20D BA89 BR92	00A89	00092	116	CDERR	MVC	PRTAREA(14),=CL14'0 **** ERROR '
000174	D249 BA97 BA96	00A97	00096	117		MVC	PRTAREA+14(74),PRTAREA+13
00017A	4EF0 RA00		00A00	118		CVD	15,DBLWORD
00017E	F327 BA98 BA00	00A98	00A00	119		UNPK	PRTAREA+15(3),DBLWORD
000184	96F0 BA9A	00A9A		120		OI	PRTAREA+17,X'F0'
				121		PUT	PRINT,PRTAREA
000196	92FF BA84	00A84		126		MVI	ERRSW,X'FF'
00019A	95FF BA86	00A86		127		CLI	BVSW,X'FF'
00019E	4780 B1A8		001A8	128		BE	RETURN
0001A2	47F0 B0D6		000D6	129	BRERR	B	COSTART
				130	*		
				131	RETURN	CLOSE	PRINT
0001B2	58D0 0004		00004	137		L	13,4(13)
0001B6	98EC D00C		0000C	138		LM	14,12,12(13)
0001BA	07FE			139		BR	14
				140	*		
0001BC	1831			141	CDTRANS	LR	3,1
0001BE	4420 B1F2	001F2		142		EX	2,TRT
0001C2	41F0 0007		00007	143		LA	15,7
0001C6	4780 B16E		0016E	144		BC	8,CDERR
0001CA	41F0 0004		00004	145		LA	15,4
0001CE	19F2			146		CR	15,6
0001D0	41F0 0006		00006	147		BNH	CDERR
0001D4	47D0 B16E		0016E	148		SR	1,3
0001D8	1B13			149		LA	15,8
0001DA	41F0 0008		00008	150		BZ	CDERR
0001DE	4780 B16E		0016E	151		BCTR	1,0
0001E2	0610			152			

LOC	OBJECT CODE	ADDR1	ADDR2	STMT	SOURCE STATEMENT
0001EC	4111 3002		00002	155	LA 1,2(1,3)
0001F0	07FE			156	BR 14
0001F2	DD00 3000 8C08		00C08	157 TRT	TRT 0(1,3),TAB
0001F8	F270 BA00 3000	00C00	00000	158 PACK	PACK DBLWORD,0(1,3)
				159 *	
0001FE	95FF BA85	00A85	00485	160 COPEDC	CLI LENSW,X'FF'
000202	9200 BA85	00A85		161	MVI LENSW,X'00'
000206	41F0 0002		00002	162	LA 15,2
00020A	4780 B16E		0016E	163	BE CDERR
00020E	5810 BA74		00A74	164	L 1,STMNT
000212	D505 1000 BBA0	C0C0C	00BA0	165	CLC 0(6,1),=C'DC=SET'
000218	4780 B2A8		002A8	166	BE DCGANG
00021C	4111 0004		00004	167	LA 1,4(1)
000220	4120 0004		00004	168	LA 2,4
000224	45E0 B1BC		001BC	169	BAL 14,CDTRANS
000228	41F0 0009		00009	170	LA 15,9
00022C	4620 B16E		0016E	171	BCT 2,CCERR
000230	1200			172	LTR 0,0
000232	41F0 000A		0000A	173	LA 15,10
000236	47D0 B16E		0016E	174	BNP CDERR
00023A	1840			175	LR 4,0
00023C	4120 0004		00004	176	LA 2,4
000240	45E0 B1BC		001BC	177	BAL 14,CDTRANS
000244	8C20 0001		00001	178	SRDL 2,1
000248	1233			179	LTR 3,3
00024A	41F0 000B		0000B	180	LA 15,11
00024E	4780 B16E		0016E	181	BNM CDERR
000252	1200			182	LTR 0,0
000254	41F0 000C		0000C	183	LA 15,12
000258	4780 B16E		0016E	184	BNP CDERR
00025C	4900 BBA6		00BA6	185	CH 0,=H'10'
000260	41F0 000D		0000D	186	LA 15,13
000264	4720 B16E		0016E	187	BH CDERR
000268	0600			188	BCTR 0,0
00026A	1834			189	LR 3,4
00026C	1A30			190	AR 3,0
00026E	5930 BA0C		00A0C	191	C 3,CDLIM
000272	41F0 000E		000E	192	LA 15,14
000276	4720 B16E		0016E	193	BH CDERR
00027A	5850 BA74		00A74	194	L 5,STMNT
00027E	D503 5000 BB80	00000	00B80	195	CLC 0(4,5),=C'BV=('
000284	4770 B2DE		02DE	196	BNE DCD
000288	92FF BA86	00A8	00A86	197 BWCD	MVI BVSW,X'FF'
00028C	5940 BA08		00A08	198	C 4,CDMAX
000290	41F0 000F		000F	199	LA 15,15
000294	47D0 B16E		0016E	200	BNH CDERR
000298	4930 B8E5		08E5	201	CH 3,INTAPE+82
00029C	4720 B16E		0016E	202	BH CDERR
0002A0	5850 BA48		00A48	203	L 5,BVLOC
0002A4	47F0 B31C		031C	204	B COSTOR
0002A8	5050 BA24		00A24	205 DCGANG	ST 5,DCLOC+12
0002AC	5050 BA34		00A34	205	ST 5,DCSET+12
0002B0	4155 000C		000C	207	LA 5,12(5)
0002B4	5050 BA1C		00A1C	208	ST 5,DCLOC+4
0002B8	5850 BA40		00A40	209	L 5,DCNQ

LOC	OBJECT CODE	ADDR1	ADDR2	STMT	SOURCE STATEMENT
0002BC	8950 0002		00002	210	SLL 5,2
0002C0	5A50 8A18		00A18	211	A 5,DCLOC
0002C4	5050 8A18		00A18	212	ST 5,DCLOC
0002C8	5850 8A08		00AC8	213	L 5,CDMAX
0002CC	5050 8A38		00A38	214	ST 5,DCSET+16
0002D0	1B55			215	SR 5,5
0002D2	5050 8A08		00AC8	216	ST 5,CDMAX
0002D6	92FF 8A87	00A87		217	MVI GANGSW,X'FF'
0002DA	47F0 80D6		00CD6	218	B CDSTART
0002DE	D503 5000 8884	00000	00884	219 DCCD	CLC 0(4,5),=C'DC=('
0002E4	41F0 0004		00004	220	LA 15,4
0002E8	4773 816E		0016E	221	BNE CDERR
0002EC	5930 8A08		00AC8	222	C 3,CDMAX
0002F0	47D0 82F8		002F8	223	BNH *+8
0002F4	5030 8A08		00A08	224	ST 3,CDMAX
0002F8	5830 8A40		00A40	225	L 3,DCNO
0002FC	5930 8A44		00A44	226	C 3,DCMAX
000300	41F0 0005		00005	227	LA 15,5
000304	4780 816E		0016E	228	BE CDERR
000308	4133 0001		00001	229	LA 3,1(3)
00030C	5030 8A40		00A4C	230	ST 3,DCNO
000310	5850 8A24		00A24	231	L 5,DCLOC+12
000314	4155 000C		0000C	232	LA 5,12(5)
000318	5050 8A24		00A24	233	ST 5,DCLOC+12
00031C	5A40 8A78		00A78	234 CDSTOR	A 4,LREC
000320	0640			235	BCTR 4,0
000322	5045 0000		00000	236	ST 4,0(5)
000326	5005 0004		00004	237	ST 0,4(5)
00032A	1222			238	LTR 2,2
00032C	4780 R342		0342	239	BZ CDCCN
000330	1B22			240	SR 2,2
000332	5025 0008		00008	241	ST 2,8(5)
000336	9500 8A86	00A86	00D06	242	CLI BVSW,X'00'
00033A	4780 80D6		00CD6	243	BE CDSTART
00033E	47F0 83C4		03C4	244	B CDEND
				245 *	
000342	5065 0008		00008	246 CDCON	ST 6,8(5)
000346	0620			247	BCTR 2,0
000348	5C26 0000		00000	248	ST 2,0(6)
00034C	1840			249	LR 4,0
00034E	4144 0001		00001	250 CNLOOP	LA 4,1(4)
000352	1824			251	LR 2,4
000354	45E0 81BC		01BC	252	BAL 14,CDTRANS
000358	5CC6 0004		0004	253	ST 0,4(6)
00035C	8C20 0001		0001	254	SRDL 2,1
000360	1233			255	LTR 3,3
000362	4740 8386		03E6	256	BM HIGHCN
000366	1824			257	LR 2,4
000368	45E0 81BC		01BC	258	BAL 14,CDTRANS
00036C	8C20 0001		0001	259	SRDL 2,1
000370	1233			260	LTR 3,3
000372	41F0 0010		00010	261	LA 15,16
000377	4780 816F		0016F	262	BNM CDERR

112

```
LOC     OBJECT CODE      ADDR1   ADDR2   STMT  SOURCE STATEMENT
000382  4740 B16E                0016E   265          BL    CCERR
000386  5906 0000                C0000   266  HIGHCN  C     0,0(6)
00038A  41F0 0012                00012   267          LA    15,18
00038E  4700 B16E                0016E   268          BNH   CDERR
000392  5006 0008                C0008   269          ST    0,8(6)
000396  4166 000C                C000C   270          LA    6,8(6)
00039A  4106 000C                C000C   271          LA    C,12(6)
00039E  5900 BA78                0A78    272          C     C,LREC
0003A2  41F0 0013                00013   273          LA    15,19
0003A6  4720 B16E                0016E   274          BH    CDERR
0003AA  1222                             275          LTR   2,2
0003AC  4780 B352                00352   276          BZ    CNLOOP
0003B0  5825 0008                CC008   277          L     2,8(5)
0003B4  5062 0000                C0000   278          ST    6,0(2)
0003B8  4166 0004                C0004   279          LA    6,4(6)
0003BC  9500 BA86        00A86            280          CLI   BVSW,X'00'
0003C0  4780 B0D6                00D6    281          BE    CDSTART
                                         282   *
                                         283  CDEND
0003CE  9500 BA84        00A84            289          CLOSE CARDIN
0003D2  4770 B1A8                001A8   290          CLI   ERRSW,X'00'
0003D6  5810 BA40                00A40   291          BNE   RETJRN
0003DA  5820 BA7C                00A7C   292          L     1,DCNO
0003DE  5012 0000                C0000   293          L     2,XREC
0003E2  8910 0002                0C002   294          ST    1,0(2)
0003E6  4101 2004                02004   295          SLL   1,2
0003EA  5000 BA60                0A60    296          LA    0,4(1,2)
0003EE  5810 BA48                0A48    297          ST    C,BVLOC+24
0003F2  5010 BA54                0A54    298          L     1,EVLOC
0003F6  5810 BA4C                0A4C    299          ST    1,EVLOC+12
0003FA  4111 0001                00001   300          L     1,BVLOC+4
0003FE  5010 BA58                0A58    301          LA    1,1(1)
000402  5810 BA78                0A78    302          ST    1,LREC
000406  4A10 B8E6                08E6    303          L     1,BVLOC+16
00040A  5810 BA58                0A58    304          AH    1,INTAPE+82
00040E  5010 BA5C                0A5C    305          S     1,5VLOC+16
000412  D21A BA89 BBE6   00A89   0BE6    306          ST    1,3VLOC+20
000418  D234 BAA4 BAA3   00AA4   0CAA3   307          MVC   PRTAREA(27),=CL27'FILE-BUILDER ERROR REPORT '
                                         308          MVC   PRTAREA+27(53),PRTAREA+26
                                                      PUT   PRINT,PRTAREA
00042C  D207 BA89 BB60   00A89   00B60   313          MVC   PRTAREA(8),=C'-CARD
000432  4140 BA91                00A91   314          LA    4,INAREA
000436  4120 000A                0000A   315          LA    2,10
00043A  4130 BAF4                00AF4   316          LA    3,INAREA+99
00043E  D209 4000 B888           C0000   317          MVC   0(10,4),=C'1234567890'
000444  8742 BA3E                0043E   318          BXLE  4,2,*-6
000448  D204 BAF7 BC01   00AF7   0DC01   319          MVC   PRTAREA+110(5),=CL7'ERROR
                                         320          PUT   PRINT,PRTAREA
00045C  92F0 BA89        00A89            325          MVI   INAREA,X'F0'
000460  9240 BA91        00A91            326          MVI   INAREA,X'40'
000464  D269 BA92 BA91   00A92   00A91   327          MVC   INAREA+1(106),INAREA
00046A  9204 BC65                00C65   328          MVI   TAB+93,X'04'
00046E  9204 BC68                00C68   329          MVI   TAB+96,X'04'
000472  9204 BC73                00C73   330          MVI   TAB+107,X'04'
000476  4800 B8E6        008E6            331          LH    0,INTAPE+82
00047A  0600                             332          BCTR  C,0
```

113

LOC	OBJECT CODE	ADDR1	ADDR2	STMT	SOURCE	STATEMENT
00047C	4200 B4CD		004CD	333		STC	0,TPMOVE+1
000480	4110 0063		00C63	334		LA	1,99
000484	1901			335		CR	0,1
000486	47D0 B48C		0048C	336		BNH	*+6
00048A	1801			337		LR	0,1
00048C	4200 B573		00573	338		STC	0,ERRMOVE+1
				339		OPEN	(GOTAPE,(OUTPUT),ERRTAPE,(OUTPUT))
00049E	5830 BA78		00A78	347		L	3,LREC
0004A2	58C0 BA10		00A10	348		L	12,CDMAXNO
0004A6	1803			349		LR	0,3
				350		GET	INTAPE
0004B2	18C1			354		LR	0,1
0004B4	4A00 BRE6		0BE6	355		AH	0,INTAPE+R2
0004B8	47F0 B4DC		04DC	356		B	TPREAD
				357	*		
0004BC	95FF BA88	0A88		358	TPSTART	CLI	EOFSW,X'FF'
0004C0	4780 B730		00730	359		BE	CLOSECUT
0004C4	5830 BA78		0CA78	360		L	3,LREC
0004C8	5820 BA3C		0A3C	361		L	2,NEXTP
0004CC	D200 3000 2000	00000	00000	362	TPMOVE	MVC	0(1,3),0(2)
0004D2	58C0 BA10		00A10	363		L	12,CDMAXNO
0004D6	1803			364		LR	C,3
0004D8	4A00 BBE6		0CBE6	365		AH	0,INTAPE+82
				366		GET	INTAPE
0004E6	5820 BA68		00A68	370		L	2,PRECNC
0004EA	4122 0001		00001	371		LA	2,1(2)
0004EE	5020 BA68		00A68	372		ST	2,PRECNO
0004F2	18C1			373		LR	0,1
0004F4	4A00 BBE6		0CBE6	374		AH	0,INTAPE+82
0004F8	955C 1000	00000		375		CLI	0(1),C'*'
0004FC	4780 R63A		0063A	376		BE	TPROC
000500	956F 1000	00000		377		CLI	0(1),C'?'
000504	4780 R63A		0063A	378		BE	TPROC
000508	9540 1000	00000		379		CLI	0(1),X'40'
00050C	4790 B518		0C518	380		BE	**12
000510	95F0 1000	00000		381		CLI	0(1),X'F0'
000514	4740 B524		00524	382		BL	TPERR
000518	46C0 B4DC		04DC	383		BCT	12,TPREAD
00051C	58C0 BA10		00A10	384		L	12,CDMAXNO
000520	92FF BA85	0A85		385		MVI	LENSW,X'FF'
				386	*		
000524	5800 BA68		00A68	387	TPERK	L	0,PRECNC
000528	1B0C			388		SR	0,12
00052A	4E00 BA00		0CA00	389		CVD	0,DBLWORD
00052E	F837 BA00 BA89	00A80	00A89	390		ZAP	CCUNT,DBLWORD
000534	92F0 BA89		00A89	391		MVI	PRTAREA,X'F0'
000538	5830 BA78		00A78	392		S	3,LREC
00053C	4133 0001		00001	393		LA	3,1(3)
000540	4E30 BA00		0CA00	394		CVD	3,DBLWORD
000544	F337 BAF8 BAFB	00AF8	00AFB	395		UNPK	PRTAREA+111(4),DBLWORD
00054A	96F0 BAFB		00AFB	396		OI	PRTAREA+114,X'F0'
00054E	5800 BA78		00A78	397		L	0,LREC
				398	ERRWRT	PUT	ERRTAPE
00055C	1821			402		LR	2,1

F01MAY72   7/27/74

PROGRAM DOCUMENTATION

LOC	OBJECT CODE	ADDR1	ADDR2	STMT		SOURCE STATEMENT	
000562	FA30 BA80 BBE5	00A80	00BE5	404		AP	COUNT,=P'1'
000568	F343 BA8A BA80	00A8A	00A80	405		UNPK	PRTAREA+1(5),COUNT
00056E	96F0 BA8E	00A8E		406		OI	PRTAREA+5,X'F0'
000572	D200 BA91 1000	00A91	00000	407	ERRMOVE	MVC	INAREA(1),O(1)
				408		PUT	PRINT,PRTAREA
000586	9240 BA89	00A89		413		MVI	PRTAREA,X'40'
00058A	D203 BAF8 BBA8	00AF8	00BA8	414		MVC	PRTAREA+111(4),=CL10' '
000590	1802			415		LR	C,2
000592	5820 BA6C		00A6C	416		L	2,BRECNO
000596	4122 0001		00001	417		LA	2,1(2)
00059A	5020 BA6C		00A6C	418		ST	2,BRECNO
00059E	46C0 C552		0C552	419		BCT	12,ERRWRT
0005A2	47F0 B48C		0048C	420		B	TPSTART
				421	*		
0005A6	9540 3000	00000		422	TPTRANS	CLI	0(3),X'40'
0005AA	4770 B5D2		005D2	423		BNE	LJUST
0005AE	4440 B634		00634	424		EX	4,CLC
0005B2	4770 B5BE		005BE	425		BNE	RJUST
0005B6	41A0 0001		00001	426	NJUST	LA	10,1
0005BA	11AA			427		LNR	10,10
0005BC	07FE			428		BR	14
0005BE	9200 BC48	00C48		429	RJUST	MVI	TAB+64,X'00'
0005C2	4113 4000		00000	430		LA	1,0(3,4)
0005C6	91F0 1000	00000		431		TM	0(1),X'F0'
0005CA	4710 B5D6		005D6	432		BC	1,*+12
0005CE	47F0 B524		00524	433		B	TPERR
0005D2	9201 BC48	00C48		434	LJUST	MVI	TAB+64,X'01'
0005D6	4440 B1F2		001F2	435		EX	4,TRT
0005DA	4773 B5EA		005EA	436		BNZ	**+16
0005DE	4440 B1F8		001F8	437		EX	4,PACK
0005E2	4FA0 CAC0		0CAC0	438		CVB	10,DBLWORD
0005E6	47F0 B604		00604	439		B	CHKTEST
0005EA	4620 B524		00524	440		BCT	2,TPERR
0005EE	1813			441		SR	1,3
0005F0	4720 B5FA		005FA	442		BP	**+10
0005F4	1BAA			443		SR	1C,10
0005F6	47F0 B604		00604	444		B	CHKTEST
0005FA	C610			445		BCTR	1,0
0005FC	4410 B1F8		001F8	446		EX	1,PACK
000600	4FA0 BA00		00A00	447		CVB	10,DBLWORD
000604	1225			448	CHKTEST	LTR	2,5
000606	4780 B62A		0062A	449		BZ	TFSTOR
00060A	4100 0008		00008	450		LA	0,8
00060E	5812 0000		00000	451		L	1,0(2)
000612	59A2 0004		00004	452	TPCHK	C	10,4(2)
000616	4740 B524		00524	453		BL	TPERR
00061A	59A2 0008		00008	454		C	13,8(2)
00061E	47C0 B62A		0062A	455		BNH	TPERR
000622	8720 B612		00612	456		BXLE	2,0,TPCHK
000626	47F0 B524		00524	457		B	TPERR
00062A	50A6 0000		00000	458	TFSTOR	ST	10,0(6)
00062F	4166 0004		00004	459		LA	6,4(6)
000632	C7FE			460		BR	14
000634	D500 3000 BBA8	00000	00BA8	461	CLC	CLC	C(1,3),=CL10' '
				462	*		

115

LOC	OBJECT CODE	ADDR1	ADDR2	STMT	SOURCE STATEMENT
00063A	11CC			463	TPROC LNR 12,12
00063C	5AC0 BA14		00A14	464	A 12,COMAXNOP
000640	9500 BA85	00A85		465	CLI LENSW,X'00'
000644	9200 BA85	00A85		466	MVI LENSW,X'00'
000648	4770 B524		00524	467	BNE TPERR
00064C	5010 BA3C		00A3C	468	ST 1,NEXTP
000650	956F 3000	00000		469	CLI 0(3),C'?'
000654	4780 B6EA		006EA	470	BE DCGP
000658	955C 3000	00000		471	CLI 0(3),C'*'
00065C	4770 B524		00524	472	BNE TPERR
000660	9503 BA87	C0A87		473	CLI GANGSW,X'00'
000664	4770 B524		00524	474	BNE TPERR
000668	5B10 BA4C		00A4C	475	S 1,BVLOC+4
00066C	5910 BA48		00A48	476	C 1,BVLOC
000670	4740 B524		00524	477	BL TPERR
000674	9869 B818		00A18	478	DCSCAN LM 6,9,DCLCC
000678	9835 7000		00000	479	LM 3,5,0(7)
00067C	45E0 B5A6		005A6	480	BAL 14,TPTRANS
000680	12AA			481	LTR 10,10
000682	4740 B524		00524	482	BM TPERR
000686	8778 B578		00678	483	BXLE 7,8,DCSCAN
00068A	9835 BA48		0CA48	484	LM 3,5,BVLCC
00068E	4166 0004		00004	485	LA 6,6(6)
000692	9879 BA54		00A54	486	LM 7,9,BVLOC+12
000696	18FC			487	LR 15,12
000698	1837			488	BVSCAN LR 3,7
00069A	45E0 B5A6		0C5A6	489	BAL 14,TPTRANS
00069E	12AA			490	LTR 10,10
0006A0	4740 B684		00684	491	BM BVEND
0006A4	8738 B69A		0C69A	492	BXLE 3,8,BVSCAN+2
0006A8	4A70 BBE6		C08E6	493	AH 7,INTAPE+82
0006AC	4A90 BBE6		008E6	494	AH 9,INTAPE+82
0006B0	46F0 B698		CC698	495	BCT 15,BVSCAN
0006B4	1816			496	BVEND LR 1,6
0006B6	5820 BA60		00A60	497	L 2,BVLOC+24
0006BA	1B12			498	SR 1,2
0006BC	8810 0002		00002	499	SRL 1,2
0006C0	0610			500	BCTR 1,0
0006C2	5012 0000			501	ST 1,0(2)
0006C6	5800 BA7C		0000C	502	L 0,XREC
0006CA	1B60			503	SR 6,0
0006CC	5800 BA7C		CCA7C	504	STH 6,GOTAPE+90
0006CC	4060 B94E		0094E	505	PUT GOTAPE
0006DA	5820 BA70		00A70	509	L 2,LRECNO
0006DE	4122 0001		00001	510	LA 2,1(2)
0006E2	5020 BA70		CCA70	511	ST 2,LRECNO
0006E6	47F0 B4BC		004BC	512	B TPSTART
				513	*
0006EA	5B10 BA38		00A38	514	DCGP S 1,DCSET+16
0006EE	47D0 B524		00524	515	BNH TPERR
0006F2	9869 BA28		00A28	516	LM 6,9,DCSET
0006F6	1299			517	LTR 9,9
0006F8	4780 B524		00524	518	BZ TPERR
0006FC	92FF BA87	00A87		519	MVI GANGSW,X'FF'
000700	9835 7000		00000	520	GPSCAN LM 3,5,0(7)

116

```
LOC      OBJECT CODE      ADDR1  ADDR2   STMT  SOURCE STATEMENT

000704   45E0 B5A6               005A6    521         BAL   14,TPTRANS
000708   12AA                              522         LTR   10,10
00070A   4740 B524               0C524    523         BM    TPERR
00070E   8778 B700               C0700    524         BXLE  7,8-GPSCAN
000712   9200 B487        00A87  004BC    525         MVI   GANGSW,X'00'
000716   47F0 B4BC               004BC    526         B     TPSTART
00071A   5810 181C               00A14    527  TPEO=  L     1,CDMAXNOP
00071E   181C                              528         SR    1,12
000720   4C10 B8E6               0C8E6    529         MH    1,INTAPE+82
000724   5A10 BA78               00A78    530         A     1,LREC
000728   92FF BA88        00A88           531         MVI   ECFSW,X'FF'
00072C   47F0 B63A               0C63A    532         B     TPROC
                                           533  CLOSEOUT CLOSE (INTAPE,,GOTAPE,,ERRTAPE)
000742   D217 BA89 BB68   00A89  00B68    543         MVC   PRTAREA(24),=CL24'ITAPE READING COMPLETED '
000748   D260 BAA1 BAA0   00AA1  00AA0    544         MVC   PRTAREA+24(97),PRTAREA+23
                                           545         PUT   PRINT,PRTAREA
00075C   D21D BA89 BBB2   00A89  0BB2     550         MVC   PRTAREA(30),=CL30'-          PHYSICAL INPUT RECORDS'
000762   5800 BA68               00A68    551         L     0,PRECNO
000766   4E00 BA00               00A00    552         CVE   0,DBLWORD
00076A   F377 BAAC BA00   00AAC  00A00    553         UNPK  PRTAREA+35(8),DBLWORD
000770   96F0 BAB3               00AB3    554         OI    PRTAREA+42,X'F0'
                                           555         PUT   PRINT,PRTAREA
000782   D20D BA91 BBD0   00A91  00BD0    560         MVC   PRTAREA+8(14),=CL14'LOGICAL OUTPUT'
000788   5800 BA70               00A7C    561         L     0,LRECNC
00078C   4E00 BA00               00A00    562         CVE   0,DBLWORD
000790   F377 BAAC BA00   00AAC  00A00    563         UNPK  PRTAREA+35(8),DBLWORD
000796   96F0 BAB3               00AB3    564         OI    PRTAREA+42,X'F0'
                                           565         PUT   PRINT,PRTAREA
0007A8   D206 BA91 BC01   00A91  0C01     570         MVE   PRTAREA+8(7),=CL7'ERROR'
0007AE   5800 BA6C               00A6C    571         L     0,ERCNO
0007B2   4E00 BA00               00A00    572         CV3   0,DBLWORD
0007B6   F377 BAAC BA00   00AAC  00A00    573         UNPK  PRTAREA+35(8),DBLWORD
0007BC   96F0 BAB3               00AB3    574         OI    PRTAREA+42,X'F0'
                                           575         PUT   PRINT,PRTAREA
0007CE   47F0 B1A8               CC1A8    580         B     RETURN
                                           581  *
                                           582  CARDIN  DC3   DDNAME=FT01F001,DSORG=PS,MACRF=GM,EODAD=CDEOF
                                           636  PRINT   DC3   DDNAME=FT06F001,DSORG=PS,MACRF=PM,RECFM=FA,BLKSIZE=133, X
                                                             LRECL=133
                                           690  INTAPE  DCB   DDNAME=FT03F001,DSORG=PS,MACRF=GM,EODAD=TPEOF
                                           744  GOTAPE  DCB   DDNAME=FT04F001,DSORG=PS,MACRF=PD,RECFM=VSB, X
                                                             BLKSIZE=2004,LRECL=4400
                                           798  ERRTAPE DCB   DDNAME=FT08F001,DSORG=PS,MACRF=PM
                                           852  *
009988                                     853  SAVE    DS    9C
00A000                                     854  DBLWORD DS    D
00A008   00000000                          855  CDMAX   DC    F'0'
00A00C   00000640                          856  CD-IM   DC    F'1600'
00A010                                     857  CDMAXNO DS    F
00A014                                     858  CDMAXNOP DS   F
00A018   0000378C                          859  DCLOC   DC    A(WORK4+4)
00A01C   00000008                          860          DC    A(WORK1)
00A020   0000000C                          861          DC    F'12'
00A024   C000CFC                           862          DC    A(WORK1-12)
00A028   0000378C                          863  DCSET   DC    A(WORK4+4)
```

PROGRAM DOCUMENTATION

LOC	OBJECT CODE	ADDR1	ADDR2	STMT	SOURCE STATEMENT
000A2C	00000D08			864		DC	A(WORK1)
000A30	0000000C			865		DC	F'12'
000A34	00000000			866		DC	F'0'
000A38				867		DS	F
000A3C						DS	F
000A40	00000000			868	NEXTP	DC	F'0'
000A44	C0000064			869	DCNO	DC	F'100'
000A48				870	DCMAX	DS	7F
000A64	00001188			871	BVLOC	DC	A(WORK2)
000A68	00000001			872	CNVEC	DC	F'1'
000A6C	00000000			873	PRECNO	DC	F'0'
000A70	00000000			874	BRECNO	DC	F'0'
000A74	000030F8			875	LRECNO	DC	A(WORK3)
000A78	000030F8			876	STMNT	DC	A(WORK3)
000A7C	00003788			877	LREC	DC	A(WORK4)
000A80	0000000C			878	XREC	DC	PL4'0'
000A84	00			879	COUNT	DC	X'00'
000A85	00			880	ERRSW	DC	X'00'
000A86	00			881	LENSW	DC	X'00'
000A87	00			882	BVSW	DC	X'00'
000A88	00			883	GANGSW	DC	X'00'
000A89				884	EOFSW	DS	CL8
000A91				885	PRTAREA	DS	CL125
000B0E	F1C9D5E3C5D9E5C9			886	INAREA	DC	CL45'INTERVIEW BEHAVIOR FILE-BUILDING PROGRAM ONE'
000B3B	404D05D2E3C9D4C2			887	HEAD	DC	CL33'(NKTIMBO) -- SEPTEMBER 15, 1973 '
				888			
000B60				889		LTORG	
000B60	60C3C1D9C4404040			890			=C'-CARD '
000B68	F1E3C1D7C540D9C5			891			=CL24'1TAPE READING COMPLETED '
000B80	C2E57E4D			892			=C'BV=('
000B84	C4C37E4D			893			=C'DC=('
000B88	F1F2F3F4F5F6F7F8			894			=C'1234567890'
000B92	F0405C5C5C5C4040			895			=CL14'0 **** ERROR '
000BA0	C4C37EE2C5E3			896			=C'DC=SET'
000BA6	000A			897			=H'10'
000BA8	40404040404040404040			898			=CL10' '
000BB2	604040404040404040C40			899			=CL30'- PHYSICAL INPUT RECORDS'
000BD0	C3D6C7C9C3C1D340			900			=CL14'LOGICAL OUTPUT'
000BDE	6040C3C1D9C440			901			=C'- CARD '
000BE5	1C			902			=C'1'
000BE6	F1C6C9D3C560C2E4			903			=CL27'1FILE-BUILDER ERROR REPORT '
000CC1	C5D9D9D6D9404040			904			=CL7'ERROR '
000CC8				905	TAB	DS	CL256
				906	*		
000008				907	WORK1	DS	300F
0011B8				908	WORK2	DS	2000F
0030F8				909	WORK3	DS	420F
003788				910	WORK4	DS	1100F
000000				911		END	TIMBO

118

PROGRAM DOCUMENTATION

RELOCATION DICTIONARY

POS.ID	REL.ID	FLAGS	ADDRESS
01	01	C8	000041
01	01	08	000045
01	01	C8	000049
01	01	08	0000B5
01	01	08	000161
01	01	08	0001AD
01	01	08	0003C9
01	01	08	000495
01	01	08	000499
01	01	08	000735
01	01	08	000739
01	01	08	00073D
01	01	08	0007F5
01	01	08	0008B5
01	01	0C	000A18
01	01	0C	000A1C
01	01	0C	000A24
01	01	0C	000A28
01	01	0C	000A2C
01	01	0C	000A64
01	01	0C	000A74
01	01	0C	000A78
01	01	0C	000A7C

PROGRAM DOCUMENTATION

CROSS-REFERENCE

SYMBOL	LEN	VALUE	DEFN	REFERENCES											
BRECND	00004	000A6C	0CE74	0416	0418				0476	0484	0486	0497			0571
BRERR	00004	0001A2	0C129	0114											
BVCD	00004	000288	00157												
BVEND	00002	0006B4	00456												
BVLOC	00004	000A48	CC871	0451											
BVSCAN	00002	000698	00488	0203	0492	0495									
RVSW	00001	00CA86	CC882	0127	0197		0296	0297	0298	0299	0301	0304	0305	0475	
CARDIN	00004	0007D4	00566	0025	0239	0242	0112	0280	0287						
CDCON	00004	000342	00246	0094											
CDCROSS	00004	00014C	001C4	0244	0100										
CDEND	00004	0003C4	00285	0063	0103	0262	0604	0144	0148	0151	0163	0171	0174	0181	0184	0187	0193	0200	0202	0221
CDEDF	00004	00015C	00110	0265	0268	0274									
CDERR	00006	00016E	00116	0056	0228										
CDLENOK	00002	0000BE	00064	0054	0065	0104									
CDLIM	00004	000A0C	00856	0191											
CDLOOP	00004	00011E	00C93	0158	0067	0069									
CDMAX	00004	000A08	00855	0213	0216	0222	0224	0363	0348	0384					
CDMAXND	00004	000A10	00857	0464	0527										
CDMAXNDP	00004	000A14	0C858	0099	0057										
CDPROC	00004	0001FE	00160	0106	0081										
CDREAD	00004	0000FA	000E1	0129	0218	0243	0281								
CDSTART	00006	0000D6	00072	02C4											
CDSTOR	00004	00031C	00234	0169	0177	0252	0258								
CDTRANS	00002	0001BC	00141	0439	0444										
CHKTEST	00002	000604	00448	0424											
CLC	00006	000634	00461	0359											
CLOSEOUT	00004	000730	00535	0276											
CNLOOP	00002	000352	00251	0270											
CNVEC	00004	00C464	00872	0072	0070	0073									
COUNT	00004	000A80	00879	0118	0119	0573	0404	0405	0390	0394	0395	0438	0447	0552	0553	0562	0563	0572
DBLWORD	00008	000A00	00854	0154	0158	0389	0390								
DCCD	00006	0002DE	00219	0156	0166	0470	0573								
DCGANG	00004	0002A8	002C5												
DCGP	00004	0006EA	00514	0205	0208	0211	0212	0230	0231	0233	0478				
DCLOC	00004	000A18	CC859	0226	0209	0225									
DCMAX	00004	000444	00870	0291											
DCNO	00004	00CA43	0C869	0483											
DCSCAN	00004	000678	CC479	0206	0214	0514	0516								
DCSET	00004	000A28	0C863	0358	0531										
EOFSW	00001	000A88	0C884	0338											
ERRMOVE	00006	000572	C04C7	0126											
ERRSW	00001	000A84	0C880	0289	0399	0541									
ERRTAPE	00004	000954	0C8C2	0345											
ERRWRT	00004	000552	00399	0419	0473	0525	0539								
GANGSW	00001	000A87	CC883	0217	0519	0506									
GOTAPE	00004	0008F4	CC748	0343	0504										
GPSCAN	00004	000700	00520	0524											
HEAD	00045	000B0E	0C887	0031	0256										
HIGHCN	00004	000386	0C266	0042	0076	0082	0092	0314	0316	0326	0327	0327		0403	0407	0493	0494	0529
INAREA	00125	000A91	0C886	0052	0061	0201	0303	0331	0351	0355	0365	0367	0374	0492
INTAPE	00004	00C894	00694	0029	0040	0537									

PROGRAM DOCUMENTATION

CROSS-REFERENCE

SYMBOL	LEN	VALUE	DEFN	REFERENCES
LJUST	00004	0005D2	00434	
LREC	00004	00CA78	0CE77	0423 0272 C302 0347 0360 0392 0397 0530
LRECNO	00004	00CA70	0CE75	0234 0509 0511 C561
NEXTP	00004	00CA3C	0C868	0361 0468
NJUST	00004	0005B6	00426	
PACK	03006	0001F8	00158	0153 0437 C446
PRECNO	00004	000A68	00873	C370 0372 0387
PRINT	00004	000834	00640	0027 0034 0C46 0038 0039 0050 0073 0074 0087 0090 0105 0105
PRTAREA	00308	000A89	00885	0031 0032 0032 0035 0117 0119 0120 0123 0306 0307 0307 0310 0313 0319 0322 0325 0391 0116 0395 0396 0405 0406 0410 0413 0414 0543 0544 0544 0547 0550 0553 0554 0557 0560 0553 0564 0567 0570 0573 0574 0577 0580 0290
RETURN	00004	0001A8	00133	0128
RJUST	00004	0005BE	00429	0425
SAVE	00008	0009B8	0CE53	0010
STMNT	00004	000A74	0C876	0077 0164 0194 0434
TAB	00256	000C08	00905	0014 0015 0015 0017 0018 0019 0019
TIMBO	00001	000000	00002	0CC8 0911
TPCHK	00004	000612	00452	0456
TPEOF	00004	00071A	00527	0712
TPERR	03004	000524	00387	0382 0433 0440 0453 0457 0467 0472 0474 0477 0482 0328 0329 0329 0330 0515 0518 0523
TPMOVE	00006	0004CC	00362	0333 0383
TPREAD	03002	0004DC	00367	0356 0378
TPROC	03002	00063A	00463	0376 0512 0526 0532
TPSTART	00004	0004BC	00358	0420 0455
TPSTOR	00004	00062A	00458	0449 0455
TPTRANS	00004	0005A6	00422	0480 0489 0521
TRT	00006	0001F2	00157	0142 0435
WORK1	00004	000DC8	0C9C7	0860 0862 D864
WORK2	00004	0011B8	0C9C8	0872
WORK3	00004	0030F8	0C9C9	0876 C877
WORK4	00004	003788	0C910	0859 C863 D878
XREC	03004	00CA7C	0CE78	0292 0502 0C17

NO STATEMENTS FLAGGED IN THIS ASSEMBLY
STATISTICS   SOURCE RECORDS (SYSIN) = 528   SOURCE RECORDS (SYSLIB) = 2803
OPTIONS IN EFFECT LIST, DECK, NOLOAD, NORENT, XREF, NOTEST, ALGN, OS, NOTERM, LINECNT = 55
688 PRINTED LINES

IV. SOURCE PROGRAM NKTIMBO

```
FORTRAN IV G LEVEL  21           MAIN           DATE = 74208          15/31/11          PAGE 0001

0001        COMMCN /PARM/ INPUT,IPRTR
0002        CALL SETUP
0003        CALL EXEC
0004        RETURN
0005        END
```

FORTRAN IV G LEVEL 21   MAIN   DATE = 74208   15/31/11

COMMON BLOCK /PAR4 / MAP SIZE 8

SYMBOL	LOCATION	SYMBOL	LOCATION	SYMBOL	LOCATION	SYMBOL	LOCATION
IPRTR	4						

SYMBOL	LOCATION
INPUT	0

SUBPROGRAMS CALLED

SYMBOL	LOCATION	SYMBOL	LOCATION	SYMBOL	LOCATION	SYMBOL	LOCATION
EXEC	98	IBCOM#	9C				

SYMBOL	LOCATION
SETUP	94

OPTIONS IN EFFECT NOID,EBCDIC,SOURCE,NOLIST,NODECK,LOAD,MAP
OPTIONS IN EFFECT NAME = MAIN , LINECNT = 50
STATISTICS SOURCE STATEMENTS = 5,PROGRAM SIZE = 282
STATISTICS NO DIAGNOSTICS GENERATED

```
FORTRAN IV G LEVEL  21            SETUP            DATE = 74208        15/31/11        PAGE 0001

        0001        SUBROUTINE SETUP
        0002        IMPLICIT INTEGER (A-Z)
        0003        DIMENSION KEYS(43),KLOC(5),KVAL(203),IDENT(18),DATAIN(2),
                   X DCTOUT(2),DTAOUT(2),CARD(20),FILTER(500),OUTF(4),A(1000),
                   X NAME(6),V(1100),TITLE(20)
        0004        INTEGER*2 PRNT(4),AGGC(4),AGGR(4),OPT(4),DIM(4),LOC(5),CHAR(5),
                   X ID(100),IF(100),D(1000),LIST(100),S(4),VN,MR
        0005        COMMON /PARM/ INPUT,IPRTR,DATAIN,NC,MC,Z,V,OUTF,PRNT,AGGC,AGGR,
                   X OPT,FILTER,ND,ID,NF,IF,A,NTF,DIM,LOC
        0006        CATA KEYS/ 1,'OUTF',4, 3,'PRIN',2,'DICT',1,'NODI',0,
                   X 4,'AGGR',2,0, 3,'OPT',2,'TWO',1,'ONE',0, 1,'INFI',4,
                   X 4,'ID',100,0, 4,'IF',100,0, 4,'DC',1,99999, 4,'RV',1,99999,
                   X 1,'N',24 /
        0007        CATA IN,OUT,INCL,EXCL,NAM /'IN  ','OUT ','INCL','EXCL','NAME'/
        0008        CATA DATA /'DATA',DTAOUT/'DATA ',DTAOUT/'DICT  '/

**********01)   IEYO38I SIZE WRN.*****************************  IEYO38I SIZE WRN.**********************************
        0009        DATA IDENT/'DESCRIPTOR VAR.     OOOOFREQ: BEHAVIOR CODE OOOOFREQ:
                   XCODE OCCC TO OOOO '/

**********01)   IEYO38I SIZE WRN.***************************************************************************
        0010        CATA CHAR/' ,-<>*VR = '/

**********01)   IEYO38I SIZE WRN.***************************************************************************

             C
             C    INITIALIZE FOR GLOBAL PARAMETERS
             C
        0011        INPUT=1
        0012        IPRTR=6
        0013        WRITE (IPRTR,1000)
        0014   1000 FORMAT ('1INTERVIEW BEHAVIOR FILE-BUILDING PROGRAM TWO',
                   X ' (TIMBO) -- SEPTEMBER 15, 1973'//'-GLCBAL PARAMETERS')
        0015        CALL SETKEY(KEYS(22),KLOC,3,0)
        0016        LOC(1)=0
        0017        F=0
        0018        DO 90 I=1,100
        0019     90 LIST(I)=I
             C
             C    CONTROL LOOP FOR GLOBAL AND LOCAL PARAMETERS
             C    TAKE FILTER AND TITLE FIRST
             C
        0020    100 READ (INPUT,1050,END=370) CARD,TITLE
        0021   1050 FORMAT (20A4,T1,20A4)
        0022        I=LYSOB(CARD,1,8C)
        0023        IF (CARD(1).EQ.NAM) GO TO 380
        0024        IF (F.GT.0) WRITE (IPRTR,1100) F
        0025   1100 FORMAT ('1LOCAL PARAMETERS FOR FILE #',I4)
        0026        L=1CO*F
```

```
FORTRAN IV G LEVEL  21                    SETUP                DATE = 74208            15/31/11              PAGE 0002

      0027          FILTER(L+1)=0
      0028          IF (CARD(1).NE.INCL.AND.CARD(1).NE.EXCL) GO TO 110
      0029          WRITE (IPRTR,1150) T TLE
      0030     1150 FORMAT ('-FILTER:'/'0',20X4)
      0031          CALL INTERP(FILTER(L-1),'I',CARD,I)
      0032          READ (INPUT,1050,END=700) TITLE
      0033      110 WRITE (IPRTR,1200) T TLE
      0034     1200 FORMAT ('-TITLE:'/'0 ,20X4)
      C
      C
      C     GET PARAMETERS (FOLLOWS DIFFERENT SETKEY FOR GLOBAL AND LOCAL)
      0035          IERR=1
      0036          WRITE (IPRTR,1225)
      0037     1225 FORMAT ('-PARAMETERS ')
      0038          CALL GETKEY(KVAL,J,6703,6700)
      0039          IF (F.GT.0) GO TO 150
      C
      C
      C     GLOBAL: RESET KEYS AND READ TAPE TO LEARN GEOGRAPHY OF RECORDS
      0040          DATAIN(1)=DATA
      0041          DATAIN(2)=IN
      0042          IF (KVAL(1).GT.0) DATAIN(2)=J
      0043          CALL SETKEY(KEYS,KLOC,4,0)
      0044          IERR=2
      0045          CALL RDPEN(DATAIN,I ,K,M,1)
      0046          IF (I.NE.0) GO TO 700
      0047          CALL RGET(DATAIN,I,Z)
      0048          IF (I.NE.0) GO TO 700
      0049          NC=V(I)
      0050          MC=V(NC+2)
      C
      C
      C     COUNT AND CHECK IDENTIFYING AND INFORMATION VARIABLES
      0051          IERR=3
      0052          K=0
      0053      120 K=K+1
      0054          IF (KVAL(K+1) 700,122,121
      0055      121 IF (KVAL(K+1).GT.NC) GO TO 700
      0056          ID(K)=KVAL(K+1)
      0057          IF (K.LT.100) GO TO 120
      0058          K=101
      0059      122 ND=K-1
      0060          IF (ND.EQ.0.) GO TO 703
      0061          WRITE (IPRTR,1250) (ID(I),I=1,ND)
      0062     1250 FORMAT ('-IDENTIFY:NC VARIABLES:'/'0',2016/(1X,2016))
      C
      0063          IERR=4
      0064          K=0
```

125

```
FORTRAN IV G LEVEL  21              SETUP              DATE = 74208        15/31/11

0065        130  K=K+1
0066             IF (KVAL(K+101)) 700,132,131
0067        131  IF (KVAL(K+101).GT.NC) GO TO 700
0068             IF(K)=KVAL(K+101)
0069             IF (K+ND.LT.100) GO TO 130
0070             IF (KVAL(K+102).NE.0) GO TO 700
0071             K=K+1
0072        132  NF=K-1
0073             IF (NF.GT.0) WRITE (IPRTR,1300) (IF(I),I=1,NF)
0074       1300  FORMAT ('-INFORMATION VARIABLES:'/'0',20I6/(1X,20I6))
           C
           C      ZERO OUT CODE CONTROL ARRAY
0075             DO 140 I=1,1000
0076        140  A(I)=0
0077             CC=C
           C
           C      CHECK AND SET FILTER
           C
0078        150  IERR=5
0079             DO 160 I=1,15
0080             IF (FILTER(L+I).GT.NC) GO TO 700
0081             IF (FILTER(L+I)) 700,162,160
0082        160  CONTINUE
0083        162  IF (I.GT.1) CALL SETADD(FILTER(L+1),V(2),LIST,NC)
0084             IF (F.GT.0) GO TO 165
0085             F=F+1
0086             GO TO 100
           C
           C      SET LOCAL PARAMETERS
           C
0087        165  IERR=6
0088             IF (KVAL(1).EQ.C) GO TO 700
0089             KVAL(1)=0
0090             AGGC(F)=0
0091             AGGR(F)=0
0092             DO 170 I=1,ND
0093             IF (ID(I).EQ.KVAL(3)) AGGC(F)=I
0094             IF (ID(I).EQ.KVAL(4)) AGGR(F)=I
0095        170  CONTINUE
0096             IF (AGGC(F).EQ.0.OR.AGGR(F).EQ.0) GO TO 700
0097             IF (AGGC(F).LT.AGGR(F)) GO TO 700
0098             OUTF(F)=J
0099             PRNT(F)=KVAL(2)
0100             OPT(F)=VAL(5)
0101             NCIM=250
0102             IF (KVAL(5).EQ.1) NDIM=40
           C
```

```
FORTRAN IV G LEVEL 21          SETUP          DATE = 74208          15/31/11          PAGE 0004

      C   GET CODE LIST BY FILE
      C
0103      IERR=7
0104      ISW=0
0105      K=0
0106      J=1
0107      C=1
0108      WRITE (IPRTR,1350)
0109 1350 FORMAT ('-BEHAVIOR CODES:'/)
      C
      C   HEAD OF SYNTAX LOOP
      C
0110  200 IF (J.LE.K) GO TO 210
0111      READ (INPUT,1050,END=700) CARD
0112      WRITE (IPRTR,1400) CARD
0113 1400 FORMAT (' ',20A4)
0114      J=1
0115      K=LYSOB(CARD,1,80)
0116  210 I=CHSCAN(CHAR,7,CARD,J,K,L)
0117      IF (I.GT.7) GO TO 700
      C
      C   OBTAIN NUMBER (IF ANY)
      C
0118      ISW=IAND(ISW,223)
0119      L=L-J
0120      IF (L.EQ.0) GO TO 220
0121      N=JCONV(CARD,J,L,P)
0122      IF (P.NE.0) GO TO 700
0123      IF (N.LT.0.OR.N.GT.999) GO TO 700
0124      ISW=IOR(ISW,32)
0125  220 J=J+L+1
0126      GO TO (270,230,240,250,260,210,210),I
      C
      C   HYPHEN
      C
0127  230 IF (IAND(ISW,10).NE.0.OR.IAND(ISW,32).EQ.0) GO TO 700
0128      ISW=IOR(ISW,8)
0129      M=N
0130      GO TO 200
      C
      C   LEFT BRACKET
      C
0131  240 IF (IAND(ISW,46).NE.0) GO TO 700
0132      ISW=IOR(ISW,4)
0133      GO TO 200
      C
      C   RIGHT BRACKET
      C
```

127

```
FORTRAN IV G LEVEL   21              SETUP        DATE = 74208        15/31/11

0134       250 IF (IAND(ISW,2).NE.0.OR.IAND(ISW,4).EQ.0) GO TO 700
0135           ISW=IOR(ISW,2)
0136           GO TO 270
                                 C
                                 C      ASTERISK
                                 C
0137       260 IF (IAND(ISW,4).NE.0) GO TO 700
0138           ISW=IOR(ISW,1)
0139           IF (IAND(ISW,32).NE.0) GO TO 270
0140           IF (IAND(ISW,14)) 700,330,700
                                 C
                                 C      CCMMA (ALL NUMBERS END UP HERE TOO)
                                 C
0141       270 IF (IAND(ISW,32).EQ.0) GO TO 700
0142           ISW=IAND(ISW,15)
0143           IF (IAND(ISW,6).NE.6.AND.IAND(ISW,2).NE.0) GO TO 290
0144           IF (IAND(ISW,8).EQ.0) GO TO 300
                                 C
                                 C      RANGE
                                 C
0145           IF (N.LT.M) GO TO 700
0146           IF (IAND(ISW,4).EQ.4.OR.C.EQ.1) GO TO 275
0147           IF (M.LE.D(CC+C-1)) GO TO 700
0148       275 I=M*4+F
0149           DO 280 L=M,N
0150           CALL IBYTE(A,I,C)
0151           IF (IAND(ISW,4).EQ.4) GO TO 280
0152           IF (C.GT.NDIM) GO TO 700
0153           D(CC+C)=L
0154           C=C+1
0155       280 I=I+4
0156           ISW=IAND(ISW,247)
0157           GO TO 310
                                 C
                                 C      LABEL BRACKETS
                                 C
0158       290 IF (C.GT.NDIM) GO TO 700
0159           IF (C.EQ.1) GO TO 295
0160           IF (N.LE.D(CC+C-1)) GO TO 700
0161       295 C(CC+C)=N
0162           C=C+1
0163           ISW=IAND(ISW,253)
0164           GO TO 320
                                 C
                                 C      SINGLE VALUE
                                 C
0165       300 I=N*4+F
0166           CALL IBYTE(A,I,C)
```

128

```
FORTRAN IV G LEVEL 21          SFTUP          DATE = 74208          15/31/11          PAGE 0006

0167        IF (IAND(ISW,4).EQ.4) GO TO 310
0168        IF (C.GT.NDIM) GO TO 700
0169        IF (C.EQ.1) GO TO 305
0170        IF (N.LE.C(CC+C-1)) GO TO 700
0171    305 C(CC+C)=N
0172        C=C+1
       C
       C  CLOSE BRACKETS
       C
0173    310 IF (IAND(ISW,6).NE.6) GO TO 320
0174        IF (CHSCAN(CHAR(5),1,CARD,J).EQ.2) GO TO 700
0175        J=J+1
0176        ISW=IAND(ISW,251)
0177    320 IF(IAND(ISW,1).EQ.0) GO TO 200
       C
       C  COMPLETE CCODES
       C
0178    330 D(CC+C)=1000
0179        IF (C.GT.1) GO TO 345
0180        IF (F.EQ.1) GO TO 700
0181        K=DIM(F-1)
0182        DIM(F)=K
0183        I=CC-K
0184        DO 335 C=1,K
0185        I=I+1
0186    335 C(CC+C)=D(I)
0187        DO 340 J=F,4000,4
0188        I=BYTE(A,J-1)
0189    340 IF (I.NE.0) CALL IBYTE(A,J,I)
0190    345 DIM(F)=C
0191        CC=CC+C
       C
       C  COMPLETE HOUSEKEEPING =CR FILE
       C
0192        LOC(F+1)=LOC(F)+(OPT(F)+DIM(F)+1)*DIM(F)+AD+NF
0193        DCTOUT(2)=OUTF(F)
0194        IER=2
0195        CALL ROPEN(CCTOUT,I,3C,1600,0,0)
0196        F=F+1
0197        IF (I) 100,100,700
       C
       C  SET UP NAME SECTION
       C
0198    370 KVAL(201)=99999
0199        KVAL(202)=99999
0200        GO TO 385
0201    380 KVAL(201)=C
0202        WRITE (IPRTR,1425)
```

```
0203      1425 FORMAT (''INAME PARAMETERS:'')
0204       385 NTF=F-1
0205           IF (NTF.LT.1) GO TO 700
0206           DO 390 K=1,ND
0207           KVAL(K+100)=K
0208       390 KVAL(K)=ID(K)
0209           IF (NF.EQ.0) GO TO 392
0210           DO 391 I=1,NF
0211           K=K+1
0212           KVAL(K+100)=K
0213       391 KVAL(K)=IF(I)
0214       392 NDF=ND+NF
0215           CALL RADIX(KVAL,NDF,4,1,4,1,KVAL(101),4)
0216           CALL BUILD(CARD,3,1,110C,1)
0217           IERR=2
0218           DO 395 F=1,NTF
0219           DCTOUT(2)=OUTF(F)
0220           CALL RPUT(DCTOUT,I,CARD)
0221           IF (I.NE.0) GO TO 700
0222       395 S(F)=0
0223           MDX=999999
0224           TYPE=2
0225           MR=1
0226           PNO=535

C
C          NAME THE DESCRIPTOR VARIABLES
C
0227       400 KD=C
0228           KD=KC+1
0229           VN=KVAL(KD)
0230           IERR=9
0231       405 IF (VN-KVAL(201)) 420,425,410
0232       410 CALL SETKEY(KEYS(33),KLOC,3,0)
0233           CALL GETKEY(KVAL(201),TITLE,&700,&415)
0234           GO TO 405
0235       415 KVAL(202)=10C000
0236       420 CALL MOVE(IDENT,1,24,NAME,1,24)
0237           N=VN
0238           N=BNBCDS(N)
0239           CALL MOVE(N,1,4,NAME,21,4)
0240           GC TO 430
0241       425 CALL MOVE(TITLE,1,24,NAME,1,24)
0242           TLOC=4*KVAL(KD+100)-3
0243       430 IF (TYPE3(CARD,VN,NAME,TYPE,TLOC,4,0,MCX,MDX,0,MR,PNO).NE.0)
0244         X GO TO 70C
0245           IFRR=2
0246           DO 440 F=1,NTF
                DCTOUT(2)=OUTF(F)
```

```
0247            CALL RPUT(DCTOUT,I,CARD)
0248            IF (I.NE.0) GO TO 700
0249      440   CONTINUE
0250            IF (KD.LT.NCF) GO TO 400
          C
          C     NAME THE ONE-WAY BEHAVIOR CODES
          C
0251            IF (KVAL(2C2).GT.99999) GO TO 450
0252            KVAL(202)=-1
0253      450   IND=C
0254            CC=1
0255            DO 450 F=1,NTF
0256      460   IF (S(F).GE.DIM(F)) GO TO 485
0257            DCTOUT(2)=OUTF(F)
0258            IERR=10
0259            VN=C(CC+S(F))
0260            IF (VN-KVAL(202)) 470,475,490
0261      470   CALL MOVE(IDENT,25,24,NAME,1,24)
0262            N=VN
0263            N=BNBCDS(N)
0264            CALL MOVE(N,1,4,NAME,21,4)
0265            GO TO 480
0266      475   CALL MOVE(TITLE,1,24,NAME,1,24)
0267      480   S(F)=S(F)+1
0268            VN=VN+1C00
0269            TLOC=(S(F)+NDF)*4-3
0270            IF (TYPE3(CARD,VN,NAME,TYPE,TLOC,4,0,MDX,MDX,0,MR,PNO).NE.0)
                X  GO TO 700
0271            IERR=2
0272            CALL RPUT(DCTOUT,I,CARD)
0273            IF (I) 700,460,700
0274      485   IND=IND+1
0275      490   CC=CC+DIM(F)
0276            IF (IND.EQ.NTF) GO TO 500
0277            IERR=10
0278            CALL SETKEY(KEYS(37),KLOC,2,0)
0279            CALL GETKEY(KVAL(2C2),TITLE,6700,&450)
0280            GO TO 450
          C
          C     NAME THE TWO-WAY BEHAVIOR CODES AND LIST DICTIONARY
          C
0281      50C   CC=C
0282            CALL MOVE(IDENT,49,24,NAME,1,24)
0283            DO 540 F=1,NTF
0284            M=DIM(F)
0285            DCTOUT(2)=OUTF(F)
0286            IF (OPT(F).EQ.0) GO TO 515
0287            VN=2C00
```

131

```
0288        TLOC=(M+NDF)*4+1
0289        DO 510 J=1,M
0290        N=D(CC+J)
0291        N=BNBCDS(N)
0292        CALL MOVE(N,1,4,NAME,12,4)
0293        DO 510 K=1,M
0294        N=D(CC+K)
0295        N=BNBCDS(N)
0296        CALL MOVE(N,1,4,NAME,20,4)
0297        IERR=11
0298        VN=VN+1
0299        IF (TYPE3(CARD,VN,NAME,TYPE,TLOC,4,0,MDX,MDX,0,MR,PND).NE.0)
0300      X   GO TO 700
0301        IERR=2
0302        CALL RPUT(DCTOUT,I,CARD)
0303        IF (I.NE.0) GO TO 700
0304  510   CONTINUE
0305  515   IF (PRNT(F).EQ.0) GO TO 535
0306        CALL LISTH
0307        CALL RCLOSE(DCTOUT,I)
0308        IF (I.NE.0) GO TO 700
0309        CALL ROPEN(DCTOUT,I,J,K,L,1)
0310        IF (I.NE.0) GO TO 700
0311  520   CALL RGET(DCTOUT,I,CARD)
0312        IF (I-1) 525,700,530
0313  525   CALL LISTD3(CARD)
0314        GO TO 520
0315  530   WRITE (IPRTR,1450) F
0316  1450  FORMAT (1-***** THE ABOVE DICTIONARY IS FCR FILE #',I3)
0317  535   CALL RCLOSE(DCTOUT,I)
0318        IF (I.NE.0) GO TO 700
0319  540   CC=CC+M
0320        RETURN
0321  C
0322  C     ERRCR MESSAGES
0323  C
0324  700   WRITE (IPRTR,1500) IERR
0325  1500  FORMAT ('1*** ERROR NUMBER',I5)
      IF (IERR.EQ.7) WRITE (IPRTR,1550) J
1550  FORMAT ('0    CARD COLUMN',I6)
      STOP 16
      END
```

132

FORTRAN IV G LEVEL 21   SETUP   DATE = 74208   15/31/11   PAGE 0010

COMMON BLOCK /PARM MAP   SIZE 2A9A

SYMBOL	LOCATION	SYMBOL	LOCATION	SYMBOL	LOCATION	SYMBOL	LOCATION	SYMBOL	LOCATION
INPUT	0	IPRTR	4	DATAIN	8	NC	10	MC	14
Z	18	V	1C	OUTF	114C	PRNT	115C	AGGC	1164
AGGR	116C	CPT	1174	FILTER	117C	ND	194C	ID	1950
NF	1A18	IF	1A1C	A	14E4	NTF	2A84	DIM	2A88
LOC	2A90								

SUBPROGRAMS CALLED

SYMBOL	LOCATION	SYMBOL	LOCATION	SYMBOL	LOCATION	SYMBOL	LOCATION	SYMBOL	LOCATION
IBCOM#	38C	SETKEY	3C0	LYSOB	3C4	INTERP	3C8	GETKEY	3CC
RCPEN	3D0	RGET	3D4	SETADD	3D8	CHSCAN	3DC	IAND	3E0
JCONV	3E4	IOR	3E8	IBYTE	3EC	BYTE	3F0	RADIX	3F4
BUILD	3F8	RPUT	3FC	MOVE	400	BABCDS	404	TYPE3	408
LISTH	40C	RCLOSE	410	L-STD3	414				

SCALAR MAP

SYMBOL	LOCATION	SYMBOL	LOCATION	SYMBOL	LOCATION	SYMBOL	LOCATION	SYMBOL	LOCATION
IN	834	OUT	838	INCL	83C	EXCL	840	NAM	844
DATA	848	F	84C	M	850	L	854	IERR	858
J	85C	K	860	N	864	CC	868	NDIM	86C
ISW	870	C	874		878	P	87C	NDF	880
MDX	884	TYPE	888	PHO	88C	KD	890	TLOC	894
IND	898	MR	89C	VH	89E				

ARRAY MAP

SYMBOL	LOCATION	SYMBOL	LOCATION	SYMBOL	LOCATION	SYMBOL	LOCATION	SYMBOL	LOCATION
KEYS	8A0	KLOC	94C	KWAL	960	IDENT	C8C	DCTOUT	C04
DTAOUT	CDC	CARD	CE4	NAME	D34	TITLE	D4C	CHAR	D9C
D	DA6	LIST	1575	S	163E				

FORMAT STATEMENT MAP

SYMBOL	LOCATION	SYMBOL	LOCATION	SYMBOL	LOCATION	SYMBOL	LOCATION	SYMBOL	LOCATION
1000	1649	1050	168D	1100	168C	1150	16DE	1200	16F2
1225	1705	1250	1715	1300	1742	1350	176F	1400	1784
1425	178D	1450	17A2	1500	17D1	1550	17E8		

OPTIONS IN EFFECT NOID,EBCDIC,SOURCE,NOLIST,NODECK,LOAD,MAP
OPTIONS IN EFFECT NAME = SETUP , LINECNT = 50
STATISTICS SOURCE STATEMENTS = 325,PROGRAM SIZE = 12166
STATISTICS 004 DIAGNOSTICS GENERATED, HIGHEST SEVERITY CODE IS 4

```
FORTRAN IV G LEVEL  21              EXEC            DATE = 74208        15/31/11

        0001          SUBROUTINE EXEC
        0002          IMPLICIT INTEGER (A-Z)
        0003          DIMENSION DATAIN(2),DTAOUT(2),FILTER(500),OUTF(4),A(1000),V(1100),
                     X R(4),S(1CG),T(12000),XREC(4)
        0004          INTEGER*2 PRNT(4),AGGC(4),AGGR(4),OPT(4),DIM(4),LOC(5),
                     X ID(100),IF(100)
        0005          COMMCN /PARM/ INPUT,IPRTR,DATAIN,NC,MC,Z,V,OUTF,PRNT,AGGC,AGGR,
                     X OPT,FILTER,ND,ID,NF,IF,A,NTF,DIM,LOC
        0006          CATA DTAOUT /'DATA    ','        '/

************011)  IEYO381 SIZE WRN.******************************************************************
        C
        C     INITIALIZATION
        C
        0007          IREC=1
        0008          DO 100 F=1,NTF
        0009          XREC(F)=0
        0010          DTAOUT(2)=OUTF(F)
        0011          LREC=(LOC(F+1)-LOC(F))*4
        0012          LBLK=LREC
        0013          IF (LBLK.LE.1000) LBLK=2000/LBLK*LBLK
        0014          CALL ROPEN(DTAOUT,I,LREC,LBLK,0,0)
        0015          IF (I.NE.0) GO TO 700
        0016          R(F)=DIM(F)
        0017     100  CCNTINUE
        0018          DO 105 I=1,ND
        0019     105  S(I)=V(ID(I)+1)
        0020          NS=ND+1
        0021          J=LOC(NTF+1)
        0022          DO 110 I=1,J
        0023     110  T(I)=0
        0024          GO TO 15C
        C
        C     HEAD OF FILE-READ LOOP
        C     CHECK GLOBAL FILTER AND SEQUENCE BREAK
        C
        0025     120  CALL RGET(DATAIN,I,Z)
        0026          IF (I-1) 125,700,240
        0027     125  I=1
        0028          IF (FILTER(1).NE.0) I=SIEVE(FILTER)
        0029          IF (I.NE.1) GO TO 120
        0030          IREC=IREC+1
        0031          MC=V(NC+2)
        0032          DO 130 J=1,ND
        0033          IF (V(ID(J)+1)-S(J)) 600,130,140
        0034     130  CONTINUE
        0035          NS=ND+1
        0036          GO TO 150
```

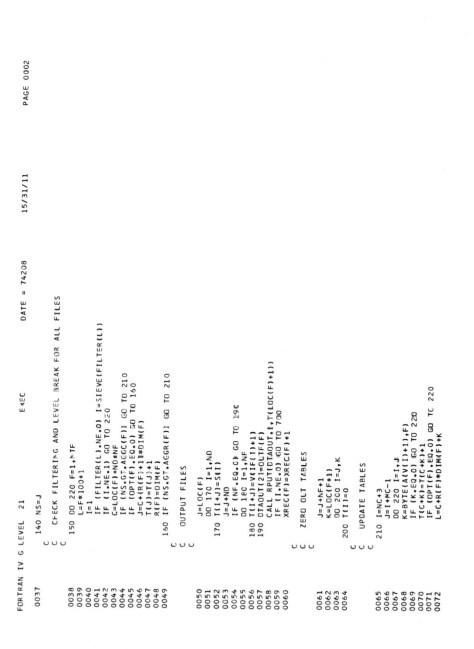

```
FORTRAN IV G LEVEL  21                    EXEC           DATE = 74208              15/31/11              PAGE 0002

0037        140 NS=J
          C
          C   CHECK FILTERING AND LEVEL BREAK FOR ALL FILES
          C
0038        150 DO 220 F=1,NTF
0039            L=F*100+1
0040            I=1
0041            IF (FILTER(L).NE.0) I=SIEVE(FILTER(L))
0042            IF (I.NE.1) GO TO 220
0043            C=LOC(F)+ND*NF
0044            IF (NS.GT.AEGC(F)) GO TO 210
0045            IF (OPT(F).EQ.0) GO TO 160
0046            J=C+(R(F)+1)*DIM(F)
0047            T(J)=T(J)+1
0048            R(F)=DIM(F)
0049        160 IF (NS.GT.AEGR(F)) GO TO 210
          C
          C   OUTPUT FILES
          C
0050            J=LOC(F)
0051            DO 170 I=1,ND
0052        170 T(I+J)=S(I)
0053            J=J+ND
0054            IF (NF.EQ.0) GO TO 190
0055            DO 180 I=1,NF
0056        180 T(I+J)=V(IF(I)+1)
0057        190 DTAOUT(2)=OLTF(F)
0058            CALL RPUT(DTAOUT,I,T(LOC(F)+1))
0059            IF (I.NE.0) GO TO 700
0060            XREC(F)=XREC(F)+1
          C
          C   ZERO OLT TABLES
          C
0061            J=J+NF+1
0062            K=LOC(F+1)
0063            DO 200 I=J,K
0064        200 T(I)=0
          C
          C   UPDATE TABLES
          C
0065        210 I=NC+3
0066            J=I+MC-1
0067            DO 220 I=I,J
0068            K=BYTE(AIV(I)+1,F)
0069            IF (K.EQ.0) GO TO 220
0070            T(C+K)=T(C+K)+1
0071            IF (OPT(F).EQ.0) GO TO 220
0072            L=C+R(F)*DIM(F)+K
```

```
0073          T(L)=T(L)+1
0074          R(F)=K
0075   220    CONTINUE
       C
       C      UPCATE PREVIOUS IDENTIFYING VARIABLE ARRAY
       C
0076          IF (NS.GT.ND) GO TO 120
0077          DO 230 I=NS,ND
0078   230    S(I)=VI(ID(I)+1)
0079          GO TO 120
       C
       C      CLOSE FILES AND MAKE REPORT
       C
0080   240    CALL RCLOSE(DATAIN,I)
0081          IF (I.NE.O) GO TO 700
0082          WRITE (IPRTR,1000) IREC
0083   1000   FORMAT ('1RUN COMPLETE',I6,'  CASES INPUT')
0084          DO 250 F=1,NTF
0085          IF (OPT(F).EQ.0) GO TO 250
0086          J=LOC(F)+ND+NF+(R(F)+1)*DIM(F)
0087          T(J)=T(J)+1
0088   250    J=LOC(F)
0089          DO 260 I=1,ND
0090          T(I+J)=S(I)
0091   260    IF (NF.EQ.0) GO TO 280
0092          J=J+ND
0093          DO 270 I=1,NF
0094          T(I+J)=VI(F(I)+1)
0095   280    DTAOUT(2)=OUTF(F)
0096          CALL RPUT(DTAOUT,I,T(LOC(F)+1))
0097          IF (I.NE.O) GO TO 700
0098          XREC(F)=XREC(F)+1
0099          WRITE (IPRTR,1050) XREC(F),F
0100   1050   FORMAT ('-',12X,I6,'  CASES OUTPUT FOR FILE',I4)
0101          CALL RCLOSE(DTAOUT,I)
0102          IF (I.NE.O) GO TO 700
0103   290    CONTINUE
0104          RETURN
       C
       C      ERROR EXIT
       C
0105   600    WRITE (IPRTR,1100) IREC
0106   1100   FORMAT ('1SEQUENCE ERROR AT CASE NO.',I6)
0107          RETURN
       C
0108   700    WRITE (IPRTR,1150) IREC
0109   1150   FORMAT ('1FATAL INPUT/OUTPUT ERROR IN EXECUTOR; CASE NO.',I6)
0110          RETURN
```

```
FORTRAN IV G LEVEL 21          EXEC          DATE = 74208          15/31/11          PAGE 0004

   0111          END
```

PROGRAM DOCUMENTATION

FORTRAN IV G LEVEL 21   EXEC   DATE = 74208   15/31/11

COMMON BLOCK /PARM / MAP   SIZE 2A9A

SYMBOL	LOCATION	SYMBOL	LOCATION	SYMBOL	LOCATION	SYMBOL	LOCATION	SYMBOL	LOCATION
INPUT	0	IPRTR	4	DATAIN	8	NC	10	MC	14
Z	18	V	1C	OUTF	114C	PRNT	115C	AGGC	1164
AGGR	116C	OPT	1174	FILTER	117C	ND	194C	ID	1950
NF	1A18	IF	1A1C	A	1AE4	NTF	2A84	DIM	2A88
LOC	2A90								

SUBPROGRAMS CALLED

SYMBOL	LOCATION	SYMBOL	LOCATION	SYMBOL	LOCATION	SYMBOL	LOCATION
RCPFN	190	RGET	194	SIEVE	198	RPUT	19C
RCLOSE	1A4	IBCOM#	1A8			BYTE	1A0

SCALAR MAP

SYMBOL	LOCATION	SYMBOL	LOCATION	SYMBOL	LOCATION	SYMBOL	LOCATION	SYMBOL	LOCATION
IREC	208	F	20C	LREC	210	LBLK	214	I	218
NS	21C	J	220	L	224	C	228	K	22C

ARRAY MAP

SYMBOL	LOCATION	SYMBOL	LOCATION	SYMBOL	LOCATION	SYMBOL	LOCATION
DTAOUT	230	R	238	S	248	T	308
						XREC	BF58

FORMAT STATEMENT MAP

SYMBOL	LOCATION	SYMBOL	LOCATION	SYMBOL	LOCATION	SYMBOL	LOCATION
1000	BF68	1050	BF8A	1100	BFAE	1150	BFCF

```
*OPTIONS IN EFFECT*  NOID,EBCDIC,SOURCE,NOLIST,NODECK,LOAD,MAP
*OPTIONS IN EFFECT*  NAME = EXEC  , LINECNT = 50
*STATISTICS*  SOURCE STATEMENTS =   111,PROGRAM SIZE =   51708
*STATISTICS*  001 DIAGNOSTICS GENERATED, HIGHEST SEVERITY CODE IS 4

*STATISTICS*  005 DIAGNOSTICS THIS STEP 2
```